GREAT LIVES (

Gerald Em

EACH VOLUME IN THE SERIES VIEWS THE CHARACTER AND
ACHIEVEMENT OF A GREAT WORLD FIGURE IN THREE PERSPEC-
TIVES—THROUGH HIS OWN WORDS, THROUGH THE OPINIONS
OF HIS CONTEMPORARIES, AND THROUGH RETROSPECTIVE
JUDGMENTS—THUS COMBINING THE INTIMACY OF AUTOBIOG-
RAPHY, THE IMMEDIACY OF EYEWITNESS OBSERVATION, AND
THE OBJECTIVITY OF MODERN SCHOLARSHIP.

JOSEPH M. LEVINE, *the editor of this volume in the Great Lives
Observed series, is Assistant Professor of History at Syracuse
University. He is the author of the forthcoming book* Humanism and History: English Historical Thought and Writing in
the Sixteenth and Seventeenth Centuries.

GREAT LIVES OBSERVED

ELIZABETH I

GREAT LIVES OBSERVED

Elizabeth I

Edited by JOSEPH M. LEVINE

*Wherein if my affection be not too great,
or my reading too small, I am of the opinion,
that if Plutarch were alive to write lives by
parallels, it would trouble him for a virtue
and fortune both, to find her a parallel
among women.*

—FRANCIS BACON

A SPECTRUM BOOK

PRENTICE-HALL, INC., ENGLEWOOD CLIFFS, N.J.

PRENTICE-HALL INTERNATIONAL, INC. (*London*)
PRENTICE-HALL OF AUSTRALIA, PTY. LTD. (*Sydney*)
PRENTICE-HALL OF CANADA, LIMITED (*Toronto*)
PRENTICE-HALL OF INDIA PRIVATE LTD. (*New Delhi*)
PRENTICE-HALL OF JAPAN, INC. (*Tokyo*)

Contents

PART THREE
ELIZABETH I IN HISTORY

GREAT LIVES OBSERVED

ELIZABETH I

Introduction

Everything about her was enigmatic. Her policies confused her enemies and puzzled her friends. Her explanations seemed invented to obscure. The language she employed was her own creation, often incomprehensible to her audience or to her correspondents. Her motives were impossible to fathom and gave rise to every kind of contrary expectation. She preferred to work— she said it herself—"underhand," rather than openly. Contemporary descriptions remain curiously external like her portraits. It is true that we know her at once, "the pale Roman nose, a head of hair loaded with crowns and powdered with diamonds, a vast ruff, a vaster fardingale, and a bushel of pearls." [1] But if we identify Elizabeth immediately we are not closer to understanding her; we know her appearance, but not her person.

Yet it is important to understand her. There is justice to the epithet Elizabethan by which we characterize the age. For almost 45 years the Queen dominated the English scene; she ruled, held court, directed policy, made (and unmade) the great, and wooed and won the rest. Somehow she transformed herself into that familiar apotheosis of the national will that is celebrated still. To learn her real motives and to know her true character is the ultimate test for the Elizabethan historian as well as for Elizabeth's biographers.

And how they have labored to discover her! The first were her contemporaries; we meet some of them below: the chroniclers Holinshed and Stow, the historians, Clapham and Camden, the memoir writers, Carey and Naunton. But close as they were to Elizabeth and as valuable in their insights, she eluded them. Perhaps they were too close, too much under her spell to stand detached and too recent to know what only the documents may tell in time, the full record of her activities. But if later historians have

[1] Horace Walpole, *Anecdotes of Painting in England,* ed. Ralph Wornum (London, 1888), I, 150.

benefited here, the confusion has remained. No one has yet surveyed the vast literature that has grown through the centuries after Elizabeth (the selection in Part Three can only begin to suggest its diversity). But it is hard not to feel that even the most convincing and recent of students have had special difficulties understanding this enigmatic lady.

Where, then, is the difficulty? It is not simply in the lapse of time. Certainly the centuries have buried much that is irretrievable, and a gulf divides us from the customs and institutions, even from the psychologies of the Elizabethans. But if many of the personalities of that age remain obscure, there are some that we may know very well. There is Elizabeth's rival Mary Stuart, the Queen of Scots, and there is Mary Tudor, her immediate predecessor. Their motives are not usually obscure, and contemporaries seem not to have had the same difficulty in deciphering them. Nor can one complain of paucity of information. Thousands of Elizabeth's letters survive, as well as speeches and documents of every description. We must look to another possibility. Elizabeth remains elusive because she deliberately intended to be so. She hid her private person behind a public façade artfully and consciously, intending to deceive or at least to hide. And she succeeded almost perfectly.

Yet that very fact is a clue to her character. To discover Elizabeth we must first unmask her—if we can. We must discover why and how she chose to conceal herself. At once, we begin to suspect the answer. Her situation was perilous and cried out for ambiguity; ambiguity accounts for much of her success. Can one doubt that frankness, honesty, impetuosity (all so helpful to the historian) would have doomed her, as they did her rival? It was a foreigner who complained, "She is a princess who can act any part if she pleases." Here is the problem in understanding Elizabeth.

The role for which she was cast was Queen of England. But she had first to play the princess. It was not an easy part; twice at least it nearly cost her much more than the crown. Each time she eluded disaster with a skill and courage that surprises us in one so young. Yet we know too little about the princess to draw conclusions too definitely. This has been the peril of her biographers. Something of the documentary evidence that would help can be presented here; the reader may draw his own conclusions. But one thing at least is clear. By Mary's reign, Elizabeth had learned to conceal herself effectively beneath an impenetrable outward show. Living very much alone, she remained aloof from conspiracy and impervious to suspicion. Outwardly at least she conformed to Catholicism and was reconciled to her sister. Her success in all this may be compared to the failure of Mary Stuart in her own reign. The Scottish Queen lost everything, too impatient to play the role for which she, like Elizabeth, had been cast.

In 1558 Elizabeth became Queen. She was 25 and a woman. To rule at all in Tudor England would have been difficult, even for a man. The Tudor monarchs had no police nor standing army. Communication and transportation were primitive; the outlying parts of the nation were remote from the authority of the court. Resistance and revolution were common enough; no theme is more frequent in the literature of the period than the perils of civil strife and political disobedience. To will policy was one thing; to implement it entirely another. The sixteenth-century ruler, whatever the theory, was dependent in fact upon popular support. Even Elizabeth's father, the most arbitrary of Tudor despots, seems to have realized this. Lack of popular support destroyed Northumberland and stymied Mary Tudor. With a sure instinct—or perhaps as the result of her valuable apprenticeship in the wings—Elizabeth seems to have known this. And she determined to make it work for her.

But she was a woman as well as a monarch and to rule thus in the sixteenth century was an almost insurmountable paradox. Custom assigned women to simple obedience. They were permitted no offices nor careers. They were even thought to bear the main responsibility for original sin. Nature and history alike were offended by the idea of the "monstrous regiment of women." English ladies had even been excluded from their rightful place in the succession. Nor did Mary Tudor's unfortunate experience bolster confidence. How was a woman to govern a nation of unruly and unwilling men?

There was but one way. Elizabeth had to turn to advantage her very deficiency. If being a woman and a ruler posed problems, there were advantages as well. From the moment she began to reign, she employed every feminine device imaginable to woo her Englishmen and win the indispensable popular support. At once, she defined her relationship with her subjects in the language of love, and for 44 years fostered a romance in which she was in turn mistress, wife, and mother. She meant it when she said late in life that she had kept the good will of her people as though they were all her husbands, ". . . for if they did not rest assured of some special love to them, they would not yield me such good obedience."

Nothing was left to chance. From the first, Elizabeth manipulated every opportunity with consummate skill. The procession before her coronation was an elaborately staged performance designed to display the young woman in all her majesty and benevolence and femininity. Nor did one need to be present to be moved; the event was soon recorded and published. But this was only the beginning; Elizabeth continued her progresses tirelessly throughout her reign, always with the same artistry and success. She visited many parts of the kingdom and was seen by many of her subjects. Ballads and narratives commemorated the occasions. The Queen had the common touch and always said the right thing. Even at the universities she charmed the learned.

Progresses were but one device for wooing the public; an endless stream of declarations and proclamations was another. Always the Queen was presented in her loving affection for her subjects, magnanimous and selfless. What a brilliant portrait of benevolent rule they combine to make! Her Parliaments gave still another opportunity. Again and again she addressed the representatives of the nation. The care with which she labored over her speeches is evident in the surviving drafts. She even revised some of them for publication. That they were successful we know; one effort became known as the "Golden Speech" and was printed long after her reign.

So Elizabeth wooed her people and artfully composed her public image. Wherever we find her she strikes a pose in a well-chosen setting. Everything was calculated. A Queen had to have her portraits. Elizabeth not only chose her artist but directed his efforts and forbade all other representations by proclamation. The finest portraitist of the age, Nicholas Hilliard, described how *he* had learned from *her!* But she framed her picture in other ways. The court was her most characteristic setting and had to be appropriately adorned. She chose the most robust courtiers to surround her, the tallest and handsomest men. Parsimonious in most ways, here she was extravagant. We are told that she owned 2000 gowns at her death. She did not invent the elaborate ceremonial, of course, but she shaped it to her own specifications. And she succeeded; her court was widely admired. It became a tourist attraction for visiting nobility, and their reports circulated abroad. Foreign ambassadors were always impressed. No doubt vanity was a motive. (Elizabeth *had* to know whether she outshone her rival Mary Stuart, for example.) But more practical concerns were involved also. Elizabeth wished to be an attractive woman; she meant also to be a respected Queen.

Most ingenious was the device she used to win the service and obedience of her courtiers. Here she encountered the problem of her femininity in its most acute form. And here it was most brilliantly surmounted. For men like Leicester, Essex, Ralegh, and the rest, submissiveness was not a natural condition. But it could be won under certain circumstances. If Elizabeth could become their lady and they the love-sick knights of chivalric tradition, awkwardness could be made to disappear and the problem of obedience might be resolved. What a grand performance this required! But Elizabeth was equal to the role until the last; at 70 she was still dancing with her young courtiers and demanding their homage and fidelity. And they responded, sometimes reluctantly, more often enthusiastically, but always extravagantly in praise of their lady, always striving for her favor and always effusive in their protestations of love and devotion. If all this seems grotesque to us, it made sense to the Elizabethans, still steeped in the literary conventions of courtly love. Needless to say the poets helped; *The Faerie Queene* was but the greatest moment in a vast literature identifying the Queen with her chivalric role.

All this has left behind its monuments: the love letters of courtiers, the reminiscences of ambassadors, the reports of travelers, the narratives of chroniclers, the ballads of the common man. Some of these may be read in the following pages. The image of the Queen, so carefully cultivated, is resplendent and obvious. But where is Elizabeth? How striking is the absence of any evidence of her private and personal life. Is this not of itself an indication of her deliberate cultivation of a public mask? How marvelously discreet she must have been that we can discover so little! There was rumor enough, of course—another pitfall for her biographers. There were some shrewd conjectures by contemporaries. But there is almost nothing from her own lips or pen. And there was no one truly intimate with her. The isolation that had been forced upon her as a princess was deliberately cultivated as a Queen. She did not marry, we know. Whatever else there was to her decision, it is obvious that marriage would have damaged her position and ruined her role. And she kept no confidants. Her ladies wrote no memoirs; her lovers—if she had them—took their secrets to the grave. Perhaps there was nothing to say. Her advisers cannot even tell us how she formulated her policies. The craftiest of men, and after half a century, the oldest of her associates, William Cecil, did not always know her mind or her motives. The Queen kept her own counsel, hid her own person, and presented herself only in a finely polished public pose.

But there were still other inducements to the Queen's performance. Policy as well as position demanded that she subordinate personal wishes to public demands. Policy encouraged deceit, made it indeed habitual in Elizabeth; dissimulation, after all, was the natural weapon for a lady in a fierce and perilous world. The Queen, for example, was her own chief diplomat. In that role she evaded, equivocated, lied; her style infuriated her enemies with its deliberate ambiguity. "With her," wrote the Spanish ambassador in 1559, "all is falsehood and vanity." He was not altogether unfair. Equivocation and ambiguity were necessary when a forthright foreign policy would have forced the hand of England's enemies. Would another policy have postponed the Armada for two decades? Then there was the problem of the succession. How she befuddled her many suitors, encouraging them against all possibility! Yet in each case we may find political reasons to suggest her motives. Once again, the perils of commitment were all too apparent. Did she ever love anyone? Did she ever think seriously of marriage? Who can say? Many have answered, of course, but the evidence is lacking. The Spanish ambassador, among others, thought he knew about the Queen's relations with Leicester. All Europe suspected much; some modern biographers have been even more certain. But the Queen's words were thoroughly ambiguous. She was ready to contradict herself as each occasion warranted. Leicester's fortunes vacillated wildly, and it is certain in any case that *he* did not know the Queen's mind. We only know that there were good political reasons for Elizabeth to keep him handy as an alternative, and there were good political reasons for her never to marry him. The inevitable mask conceals the rest.

If foreign policy and the succession demanded dissimulation, so also did religion. Once again, the Queen's skill in creating ambiguity is remarkable. What did she believe in her own conscience? The question is almost irrelevant. Her policy again masks her feelings. She worshipped regularly, composed prayers, and invariably invoked Providence for her policies. Protestant born, Catholic under Mary, Protestant again in her own reign, she nevertheless kept a crucifix and lighted taper in her own chapel to confound the Puritans and keep Catholic expectations alive. The Papal Bull of excommunication was thus delayed until 1570. She would not search consciences, she said, and her own is quite beyond our reach.

What then is left to say of this woman who so carefully concealed herself? A few definite things only perhaps. There is, for example, no mistaking Elizabeth's will and intelligence, nor her desire and love of rule. There is no avoiding her deviousness nor her discretion. Most importantly, and whatever her other qualities, we recognize always her self-control and her self-discipline. Even in her diet, she was ascetic. She avoided all the temptations of self when they conflicted with her chosen role. She subordinated her whims to the necessities of her rule. She knew others well and made few mistakes in estimating their characters, but few knew her or judged her rightly. If her traits were not the most endearing, they at least demanded respect. And if recognizing them leaves us still uneasily on the exterior of her person—that is somehow precisely where she wished us to be.

The documents for Elizabeth's reign are copious. They tell us much about what she said and about what she did. Unfortunately, most of her pronouncements were official; there are, for example, relatively few personal letters. These may be supplemented, however, by the reports of her conversations that appear in the letters of others, in ambassadors' dispatches, and in memoirs. Often these dialogues reveal the Queen better than her formal statements; sometimes, indeed, they capture her in an altogether unguarded moment. Naturally they must be used with caution; they do not have the primary authority of the Queen's words directly, and were often recalled only long afterward. In the selections offered here, many snatches of conversation are reported along with a representative sample of Elizabeth's letters and speeches. A historian and biographer of Elizabeth, Sir John Neale, also considers some of the problems in interpreting the anecdotal material. Although more could be said about the problem of authenticity, the student will at least be alerted to the difficulties.

Elizabeth's actions were as important as her words. Indeed, they are often more reliable clues to her character than her elaborately calculated language. But here the full context of each of her decisions must be known before it can be understood. And here, undoubtedly, our documents are most restricted. All that can be done is to suggest some of the Queen's most characteristic problems and something of her response to each. There are no shortcuts; only by detailed study and the full record can one hope to discover from her deeds Elizabeth's true motivation. But at least the main problems may be introduced.

There is, finally, a third category of evidence to help to estimate the Queen. We may try to view her through the eyes of her contemporaries. A number of first-hand descriptions—most friendly, a few hostile—are also presented here. Needless to say, they too must be read with caution; we must always consider the reporter as well as the report. But these narratives are obviously useful, and their different vantage points necessary for a well-rounded picture.

The plan of the book, then, is to show Elizabeth first as she confronted her roles as Princess and Queen; next as she is revealed in some contemporary views at different stages in her career. Her approaches to the special problems of her reign: religion, foreign policy, the succession, etc., follow. The views of some representative historians and biographers from the seventeenth century to the present form the conclusion. All documents have been drawn from printed sources, modernized somewhat in spelling and punctuation. The multiple perspectives here afforded the student will probably not settle any issues; but it is hoped that they will at least show the way.

Chronology of the Life of Elizabeth I

1533	(September 7) Born at Greenwich Palace, daughter of King Henry VIII and Anne Boleyn.
1536	Anne Boleyn beheaded on the charge of adultery.
1544–49	Tutored by William Grindall and Roger Ascham.
1547	Henry VIII dies; Edward VI succeeds.
1549	Seymour affair; Elizabeth suspected.
1553	Edward VI dies; Mary succeeds.
1554	Wyatt's rebellion; Elizabeth's imprisonment in the Tower and confinement at Woodstock.
1558	(November 17) Mary dies; Elizabeth succeeds.
1559	(January 15) Coronation.
1559	Treaty of Château Cambresis. Acts of Supremacy and Uniformity; Protestant Rebellion in Scotland; Elizabeth aids the rebels covertly.
1560	Treaty of Edinburgh, Mary Stuart returns to Scotland. Death of Amy Robsart (Robert Dudley's wife).
1562	Huguenot Wars begin.
1565	Mary Stuart marries Darnley against Elizabeth's will.
1566	(June 19) James VI born.
1567	Darnley murdered. Mary marries Bothwell, is defeated and forced to flee to England where she remains a captive of Elizabeth.
1569	Northern rebellion suppressed.
1570	Rebellion of Leonard Dacre. Elizabeth excommunicated by the Pope.
1571	Ridolfi conspiracy exposed.
1572	Norfolk executed. Massacre of St. Bartholomew's day.
1577	Revolt in the Netherlands.
1579–82	Duke of Alençon courts Elizabeth unsuccessfully.
1581	Elizabeth supports Don Antonio of Portugal against Philip II. Campion executed.
1583–84	Throckmorton plot exposed.
1585–87	Leicester in the Netherlands.

1586	Babington conspiracy; Mary's trial.
1587	Mary Stuart executed.
1588	Spanish Armada defeated and dispersed. Leicester dies.
1588–98	The Apogee of the reign.
1598	Death of Burghley. Death of Philip II. Irish revolt begins.
1601	Essex rebellion and execution. Monopolies debate in Parliament and "Golden Speech."
1603	(March 24) Elizabeth dies.

PART ONE

ELIZABETH I VIEWED BY HER CONTEMPORARIES

1

Early Years

Descriptions of the Princess by contemporaries are scarce. Nor is this surprising; after her mother's execution in 1536 she necessarily left the center of the stage and lived in relative obscurity, first in the shadow of her younger brother, then of Mary. Still her portrait was drawn for us on several occasions and if the descriptions are tantalizing they have been fully—perhaps too fully—exploited by her biographers. Here are some of the most famous.

There are several descriptions of Elizabeth's birth and christening. The fullest perhaps was by the London citizen and chronicler Edmund Hall.

The seventh day of September [1533], being Sunday, between three and four of the clock at afternoon, the Queen was delivered of a fair lady, which day the Duke of Norfolk came home to the christening, and for the Queen's good deliverance, *Te Deum* was sung. . . .

The Wednesday following . . . the Mayor, Sir Stephen Pecock, in a gown of crimson velvet . . . the aldermen in scarlet with collars and chains, and all the council of the city with them, took their barge . . . and so rowed to Greenwich where there were many lords, knights, and gentlemen assembled. All the walls between the King's Palace and the Friars were hanged with arras, and all the way strewn with green rushes. . . . When all these things were ordered, the child was brought to the hall, and then every man set forward: first the citizens two and two, then gentlemen, esquires and chaplains, next after them aldermen, and the Mayor alone; next . . . the King's council, the King's Chaplain in copes; then barons, bishops, earls; then came the Earl of Essex . . . the Marquis of Exeter . . . the Marquis Dorset . . . the Lady Mary of Norfolk. . . . The old Duchess of Norfolk bore the child in a mantle of purple velvet with a long train furred with ermine. . . . The Countess of Kent bore the long train of the child's mantle. . . . In the midst over the said child was borne a canopy. . . . When the child was come to the church door, the Bishop of London met it with divers bishops and abbots mitred and began the observances of the sacraments. The Godfather was the Lord Archbishop of Canterbury, the Godmothers were the old Duchess of Norfolk and the old Marchioness of Dorset, widows, and the child was named Elizabeth. And after everything was done, the child was brought to the font and christened and this done, the Garter Chief King of Arms cried aloud, "God of his infinite goodness, send prosperous life and long, to the high and mighty Princess of England, Elizabeth." And then the trumpets blew. . . .[1]

Hall's account contrasts with the hostile account of Eustace Chapuys, the Imperial Ambassador.

. . . On Sunday last, on the eve of Lady Day, about three o'clock in the afternoon, the Queen . . . was delivered of a girl, to the great disappointment and sorrow of the King, of the Lady herself, and of others of her party, and to the great shame and confusion of physicians, astrologers, wizards, and witches, all of whom affirmed that it would be a boy . . .

*   *   *

It must, therefore, be concluded that God has entirely abandoned this King, and left him a prey to his own misfortune, and to his

[1] From *Hall's Chronicle*, ed. Henry Ellis (London, 1809), pp. 805–6.

obstinate blindness, that he may be punished and completely
ruined. Indeed there is already every appearance of this, . . . if
we consider the almost general indignation which this, the King's
second marriage, and consequent acts have produced among the
people, both high and low . . .[2]

*Elizabeth's childhood was marked by many startling changes
of fortune. As Henry VIII exchanged Queens and religious
positions, Elizabeth's situation fluctuated. Her mother, Anne
Boleyn, was executed in 1536 and Elizabeth was declared
illegitimate by Act of Parliament. The successions of her
Protestant brother Edward VI (1547) and her Catholic sister
Mary Tudor (1553) only served to keep her prospects uncertain. Yet Elizabeth was not neglected; during these years she
was befriended by many. And she received a remarkable education in the new and fashionable learning of humanism. Here,
in 1550, her tutor, Roger Ascham, the author of a well-known
educational treatise,* The Schoolmaster, *boasts of her progress
to a continental friend.*

The Lady Elizabeth has accomplished her sixteenth year; and
so much solidity of understanding, such courtesy united with
dignity, have never been observed at so early an age. She has the
most ardent love of true religion and of the best kind of literature.
The constitution of her mind is exempt from female weakness, and
she is endowed with a masculine power of application. No apprehension can be quicker than hers, no memory more retentive.
French and Italian she speaks like English; Latin, with fluency,
propriety, and judgment; she also spoke Greek with me, frequently,
willingly, and moderately well. Nothing can be more elegant than
her handwriting, whether in the Greek or Roman character. In
music she is very skillful, but does not greatly delight. With respect
to personal decoration, she greatly prefers a simple elegance to show
and splendor, so despising "the outward adorning of plaiting the

[2] From *Calendar of State Papers Spanish Henry VIII* (London, 1882), **IV, ii,**
789-90.

hair and of wearing of gold," that in the whole manner of her life she rather resembles Hippolyta than Phaedra.

She read with me almost the whole of Cicero, and, a great part of Livy: from these two authors, indeed, her knowledge of the Latin language has been almost exclusively derived. The beginning of the day was always devoted by her to the New Testament in Greek, after which she read select orations of Isocrates and the tragedies of Sophocles, which I judged best adapted to supply her tongue with the purest diction, her mind with the most excellent precepts, and her exalted station with a defence against the utmost power of fortune. For her religious instruction, she drew first from the fountains of Scripture, and afterwards from St. Cyprian, the "Common places" of Melancthon, and similar works which convey pure doctrine in elegant language. . . . By diligent attention to these particulars, her ears became so practised and so nice, that there was nothing in Greek, Latin, or English, prose or verse, which, according to its merits or defects, she did not either reject with disgust, or receive with the highest delight . . .[3]

However, two incidents in these years brought the Princess real peril. In the first (1548) Elizabeth became involved with the Protector Somerset's brother, Thomas Seymour, Lord Admiral of England. Seymour had ambitions that threatened his brother's rule and led ultimately to his trial and execution for treason. He tried to use Elizabeth to further his ambitions, courting the young girl and thus implicating her in his plans. How far he succeeded in winning Elizabeth's affection remains conjectural, but the incident undoubtedly impressed upon her the need for restraint and caution, qualities afterward much responsible for her success as Queen. Dangerous as was this incident, she suffered even more suspicion in the rebellion of Thomas Wyatt against her sister Mary Tudor (1554). Wyatt had hoped to match Elizabeth with Edward Courtenay and set her on the throne of England. Was Elizabeth implicated? Once again, her own caution and the loyalty of her friends (Wyatt absolved her at his execution) left no evidence. The

[3] From Lucy Aikin, *Memoirs of the Court of Queen Elizabeth* (London, 1818), I, 95–96.

*Protestant historian John Foxe tells the story of her imprison-
ment at this time, heightening perhaps, but not exaggerating,
the danger and loneliness of the young woman.*

"God's Providence in Preserving the Lady Elizabeth in Queen Mary's Days" [4]

After this it happened, immediately upon the rising of Sir
Thomas Wyatt . . . the Lady Elizabeth and Lord Courtenay were
charged with false suspicion of Sir Thomas Wyatt's rising. Whereupon Queen Mary . . . being offended with the said Lady Elizabeth . . . the next day after the rising of Wyatt sent to her three
of her counsellors . . . with their retinue and troop of horsemen
. . . who, at their sudden and unprovided coming, found her at
the same time sore sick in her bed. . . . They burst into her chamber, unbidden. Her Grace being not a little amazed said unto them,
"My lords, is the haste such, that it might not have pleased you
to come tomorrow in the morning?" . . . Whereunto they answered, that they came from the Queen to do their message and
duty, which was to this effect, that the Queen's pleasure was that
she should be at London, the seventh day of the present month.
. . . "Our commission is such, and so straineth us, that we must
needs bring you with us, either quick or dead." . . .

* * *

Now when she came to court, her Grace was there straightways
shut up, and kept as close prisoner a fortnight, seeing neither King
nor Queen, nor lord nor friend, all that time. . . . The Friday before Palm Sunday, the Bishop of Winchester Stephen Gardiner with
nineteen other of the Council came unto her Grace and burdened
her with Wyatt's conspiracy, which she utterly denied. . . . After
long debating of matters, they declared unto her that it was the
Queen's will and pleasure that she should go unto the Tower, while
the matter was further tried and examined. . . .

Palm-Sunday about nine of the clock, two lords returned again,

[4] From John Foxe, *The Acts and Monuments,* ed. Joseph Pratt (London, 1877),
VIII, 606–21.

declaring that it was time for her Grace to depart. She answered, "If there be no remedy, I must be contented," willing the lords to go before. . . . In the meantime commandment was given in all London, that everyone should keep the church, and carry their palms, while in the mean season she might be conveyed without all recourse of people into the Tower.

. . . At landing she first stayed, and denied to land at those stairs where all traitors and offenders customarily used to land. . . . The lords were gone out of the boat before and asked why she came not. One of the lords went back again to her, and brought word she would not come. . . . Another because it did then rain, offered to her his cloak which she putting it back with her hand with a good dash refused. So she coming out, having one foot upon the stair, said, "Here landeth as true a subject, being prisoner, as ever landed at these stairs; and before thee, Oh God, I speak it, having no friends but thee alone." To whom the said lord answered again, that if it were so, it was the better for her. . . .

[*At length, Elizabeth was removed from the Tower to close confinement at Woodstock. Foxe continues.*]

. . . During the imprisonment of this lady and princess . . . divers were examined, and divers offers made to them to accuse the guiltless lady, being in her captivity. Howbeit, all that notwithstanding, no matter could be proved by all examinations. . . . Whereupon the Lady Elizabeth, at her departing out from Woodstock, wrote these verses with her diamond in a glass window.

> Much suspected by me:
> Nothing proved can be.
> > Quoth Elizabeth, prisoner.

Thus this worthy lady, oppressed with continual sorrow, could not be permitted to have recourse to any friends she had, but still in the hands of her enemies was left desolate, and utterly destitute of all that might refresh a doleful heart, fraught full of terror and thraldom. Whereupon no marvel if she, hearing upon a time, out of her garden at Woodstock, a certain milkmaid singing pleasantly, wished herself to be a milkmaid as she was; saying that her case was better, and life more merry than was hers, in that state she was.

[*Elizabeth was brought at last to court where*] the Queen sent for her Grace at ten of the clock in the night to speak with her: for she had not seen her in two years before. Yet, for all that, she was amazed at the so sudden sending for, thinking it had been worse for her than afterwards it proved, and desired her gentlemen and gentlewomen to pray for her; for that she could not tell whether ever she should see them again or no. . . Mistress Clarencius conducted her to the Queen's bed-chamber, where her Majesty was. At the sight of whom her Grace kneeled down, and desired God to preserve her Majesty, not mistrusting but that she should try herself as true a subject towards her Majesty, as ever did any; and desired her Majesty even so to judge of her; and said, that she should not find her to the contrary, whatsoever report otherwise had gone of her. To whom the Queen answered, "You will not confess your offence, but stand stoutly in your truth: I pray God it may so fall out." "If it doth not," quoth the Lady Elizabeth, "I request neither favor nor pardon at your Majesty's hands." "Well," said the Queen, "you stiffly still persevere in your truth. Belike you will not confess but that you have been wrongfully punished." "I must not say so, if it please your Majesty, to you." "Why then," said the Queen, "belike you will to others." "No, if it please your Majesty," quoth she, "I have borne the burden and must bear it. I humbly beseech your Majesty to have a good opinion of me, and to think me to be your true subject, not only from the beginning hitherto, but forever, as long as life lasteth." And so they departed with very few comfortable words of the Queen, in English: but what she said in Spanish, God knoweth. It is thought that King Philip was there behind a cloth, and not seen, and that he showed himself a very friend in the matter.

By 1557 Elizabeth's fortunes were improving. The Venetian ambassador, Giovanni Michieli, who had been in England for three years, describes her situation and her person on the eve of her accession.

[*Queen Mary's anxiety*] which proceeds from hatred, is owing to her evil disposition towards her sister, my Lady Elizabeth. Although she dissembles, it cannot be denied that she displays in many ways the scorn and ill will she bears her; the Queen, whenever she sees her, fancies herself in the presence of the affronts and ignominious treatment to which she was subjected on account of her mother, from whom in great part the divorce from Queen Catherine originated. But what disquiets her most of all is to see the eyes and hearts of the nation already fixed on this lady as successor to the Crown. . . . Besides this, the Queen's hatred is increased by knowing her to be averse to the present religion, she having not only been born in the other, but being versed and educated in it; for although externally she showed, and by living catholically shows, that she has recanted, she is nevertheless supposed to dissemble, and to hold to it more than ever internally.

Of this sister of hers I must remind your Serenity that after the repudiation of Queen Catherine (the present Queen's mother) she was born of Henry VIII and of his second wife Anne Boleyn, an Englishwoman and of noble birth, although two [actually three] years afterwards she was beheaded for adultery. My Lady Elizabeth was born in September 1533, so she is now 23 years old. She is a young woman, whose mind is considered no less excellent than her person, although her face is comely rather than handsome, but she is tall and well formed, with a good skin, although swarthy; she has fine eyes and above all a beautiful hand of which she makes display; and her intellect and understanding are wonderful, as she showed very plainly by her conduct when in danger and under suspicion. As a linguist she excels the Queen for besides Latin she has no slight knowledge of Greek, and speaks Italian more than the Queen does, taking so much pleasure in it that from vanity she will never speak any other language with Italians. She is proud and haughty, as although she knows that she was born of such a mother, she nevertheless does not consider herself of inferior degree to the Queen, whom she equals in self-esteem; nor does she believe herself less legitimate than her Majesty. . . . She prides herself on her father and glories in him; everybody saying that she also resembles him more than the Queen does; and he therefore always liked her and had her brought up in the same way as the Queen, and bequeathed to each of them 10,000 scudi per annum, and, what matters more, substituted her in the stead of the Queen as successor to the Crown, should he die without male heirs. She now lives upon this settlement from her father, but is always in debt, and would be much more so did she not steadily restrain herself to avoid any increase of the Queen's hatred and anger; either by increasing the number of gentlemen and servants of her household, or by adding to her expenditure in any other way; and here I may add that there is not a lord or gentleman in the kingdom who has failed, and continues endeavoring, to enter her service himself or to place one of his sons or brothers in it, such being the love and affection borne her. When requested to take servants she always excuses herself on account of the straits and poverty in which she is kept, and by this astute and judicious apology she adroitly incites a tacit compassion for herself and consequently yet greater affection, as it seems strange and vexatious to everybody that being the daughter of a King she should be treated and acknowledged so sparingly. Since Wyatt's rebellion she may be said never to have been at liberty, for although she is allowed to live at a house of hers called Hatfield, 12 miles from London, the Queen has nevertheless many spies and guards in the neighborhood who keep strict watch on all persons passing to and fro, nor is anything said or done that is not immediately reported to the Queen, so she is obliged to act very cautiously.

At the time of the Queen's pregnancy, Lady Elizabeth, when made to come to the court, contrived so to ingratiate herself with all the Spaniards, and especially with the King, that ever since no one has favored her more than he does; for not only would he not permit, but opposed and prevented the Queen's wish to have her disinherited and declared a bastard by Act of Parliament, and consequently ineligible to the throne which, besides affection, implies some particular design on the part of the King with regard to her. His Majesty also dissuaded and prevented the Queen from sending her out of the kingdom, to Spain or elsewhere, as she wished to do. From this, your Serenity can comprehend what the Queen thinks of her, for there is no doubt whatever but that had not her Majesty been restrained by the King, and by the fear of some insurrection, she for any trifling cause would gladly have inflicted every sort of punishment on her; so great is the effect produced by recollection, not only of past offences but also of present ones, for it unfortunately appears that never is a conspiracy discovered in which either justly or unjustly she or some of her servants are not mentioned. But the respects to which I have alluded hold the Queen's hand, and having no suitable cause to proceed against her, she dissembles her hatred and anger as much as she can, and endeavors when they are together in public to receive her with every sort of graciousness and honor, nor does she ever converse with her about any but agreeable subjects. Such is the position of my Lady Elizabeth. . . .[5]

By 1558, Mary was dying and Elizabeth's accession was at hand. Long afterward Thomas Markham recalled having given assistance to Elizabeth at that time.

He did never forsake her royal person when her Highness was in any supposed danger, as did appear in the last year of Queen Mary, when he had in his charge 300 footmen in the town of Berwick; and upon the dangerous sickness of her dear sister, it pleased her Majesty through Mr. Parry her Cofferer, to signify to him that he should with all convenient speed repair to Brocket Hall, leaving his own band with such other captains as he could trust to be in readiness with their bands likewise to serve for the maintenance of her royal estate, title and dignity. This he performed faithfully and brought the captains' names signed with their own hands, by which they vowed their dutiful forwardness to adventure their lives in her Majesty's service with 10,000 men. At which time he received her gracious and favorable thanks for the same.[6]

[5] From *Calendar of State Papers Venetian* (London, 1884), VI, 1058–60.
[6] From *Calendar of the Manuscripts of the Marquis of Salisbury at Hatfield House* (London, 1892), IV, 189.

2
The Accession

The young woman who became Queen in 1558 might well have been filled with apprehension. The problems that beset the nation were overwhelming. Oscillations of rule and policy had bred confusion and uncertainty. But chief among Elizabeth's difficulties was her own person. As a woman ruler, Elizabeth appeared an anomaly. No precedents could sanction a relationship that reversed the customary (or as sixteenth-century men supposed it, the natural) order of things. But, to the outward world, Elizabeth showed no signs of hesitation or uneasiness. Even as she rode to her coronation, she showed the public character that would override all such objections. That she could turn her femininity to positive advantage was one of her most remarkable achievements; it had certainly not helped her sister nor would it aid her rival, Mary Stuart.

In 1558, just prior to Elizabeth's accession, two Protestants abroad, John Knox and Christopher Goodman, chose to write works condemning feminine (i.e., Marian) rule. Knox called his work, The First Blast of the Trumpet Against the Monstrous Regiment of Women. *He argued that feminine rule was "repugnant to nature, contumely to God, and the subversion of good order, equity and justice." When the Protestant Elizabeth succeeded Mary, both men were embarrassed. Even their mentor, John Calvin, sought to intercede from Geneva, writing to William Cecil on January 1, 1559.*

. . . Two years ago, John Knox asked of me, in a private conversation, what I thought about the government of women. I candidly replied, that as it was a deviation from the original and proper order of nature, it was to be ranked, no less than slavery, among the punishments consequent upon the fall of man; but that there were occasionally women so endowed, that the singular good qualities which shone forth in them, made it evident that they were raised up by divine authority; either that God designed by such examples to condemn the inactivity of men, or for the better setting forth his own glory. I brought forward Huldah and Deborah; and added, that God did not vainly promise by the mouth of Isaiah, that queens should be the nursing mothers of the church; by which prerogative it is very evident that they are distinguished from females in private life. I came at length to this conclusion, that since both by custom and public consent and long practice it has been established, that realms and principalities may descend to females by hereditary right, it did not appear to me necessary to move the question, not only because the thing would be invidious, but because in my opinion it would not be lawful to unsettle governments which are ordained by the peculiar providence of God. I had no suspicion of the book, and for a whole year was ignorant of its publication. When I was informed of it by certain parties, I sufficiently showed my displeasure that such paradoxes should be published; but as the remedy was too late, I thought that the evil which could not now be corrected, should rather be buried in oblivion than made a matter of agitation.[1]

> *Even Elizabeth's defenders found her femininity a problem.*
> *Here John Aylmer answers Knox. His apology reveals the*
> *difficulty that would beset the Queen in marriage.*

Yea say you, God hath appointed her to be subject to her husband. Therefore she may not be the head. I grant that so far as pertaineth to the bands of marriage and the office of a wife, she must be a subject. But as a Magistrate she may be her husband's head, for the Scripture saith not thine eye must be to the man but to thy husband. Neither oweth every women obedience to every man but to her own husband. Well if she be her husband's subject she

[1] From *The Zurich Letters*, 2nd series, ed. H. Robinson (London, 1845), pp. 34–35.

can be no ruler, that followeth not. For the child is the father's subject and . . . may be by law a head, yea the head of his father and his father subject. Why may not the woman be the husband's inferior in matters of wedlock, and his head in the guiding of the commonwealth?

. . . Men will not stand in awe so much of a woman as of a man; that is their fault and not hers. No more will they of a child and yet be they traitors that do disobey him.[2]

Still most Englishmen welcomed the Queen whatever their reservations. A flood of ballads illustrates the popular, or at least the Protestant mood. Here is one example. It begins with a long description of how God punished the English people under Mary for their contempt, and then continues:

Yet God as God, still always one
    Though angry, yet began to stay,
Plaguing the realm and people each one,
    At last with tears began to say:
Oh England! England! sure dost thou stray,
My martyrs blood shed out this day,
      In woeful plight!
The infants young that fatherless be,
With widows poor crying to me,
      Withdraws my spite.

With that the skies their hue did change
    And light outshone in darkness stead;
Up, said this God with voice not strange,
    Elizabeth, this realm now guide!
    My will in thee do not thou hide,
    And vermin dark let not abide
      In this thy land!
Straightway the people out did cry,
Praised be God and God save thee,
      Queen of England! [3]

[2] From John Aylmer, *An Harborowe for Faithful Subjects* (Strassburg, 1559), pp. 16–17.
[3] From John Audeley, *The Wonders of England*, in *A Collection of Black-Letter Ballads . . . 1559–97*, ed. Joseph Lilly (London, 1867) pp. 94–97.

Elizabeth took full advantage of the popular mood. The day before her coronation she paraded through London, exhibiting from the first all those arts that were to capture and hold the popular imagination. An account of the procession was printed at once and circulated. A brief extract only can be given here.

Upon Saturday, which was the 14th day of January, in the year of our Lord God 1558, about two of the clock at afternoon, the most noble and Christian Princess, our most dread Sovereign Lady Elizabeth, by the grace of God, Queen of England, France, and Ireland, Defender of the Faith, etc., marched from the Tower, to pass through the City of London toward Westminster, richly furnished, and most honorably accompanied, as well with gentlemen, barons, and the other nobility of this realm, as also with a notable train of goodly and beautiful ladies, richly appointed. And entering the City was of the people received marvelous entirely, as appeared by the assembly, prayers, wishes, welcomings, cries, tender words, and all other signs, which argue a wonderful earnest love of most obedient subjects toward their sovereign. And on the other side, her Grace, by holding up her hands, and merry countenance to such as stood far off, and most tender and gentle language to those that stood nigh to her Grace, did declare herself no less thankfully to receive her people's good will, than they lovingly offered it unto her. To all that wished her Grace well, she gave hearty thanks, and to such as bade God save her Grace, she said again, God save them all, and thanked them with all her heart: so that on either side there was nothing but gladness, nothing but prayer, nothing but comfort. . . .

* * *

At the Standard in Cheape, which was dressed fair against the time, was placed a noise of trumpets, with banners and other furniture. The cross likewise was also made fair and well trimmed, and near unto the same, upon the porch of Saint Peter's church door, stood the waits[4] of the City, which did give a pleasant noise with

[4 A member of a small body of instrumentalists maintained by a city or town at public expense.]

their instruments as the Queen's Majesty did pass by, which on every side cast her countenance, and wished well to all her most loving people. Soon after that her Grace passed the Cross, she had espied the pageant erected at the Little Conduit in Cheape, and incontinent required to know what it might signify. And it was told her Grace, that there was placed Time. "Time," quoth she, "and Time hath brought me hither." And so forth the whole matter was opened to her Grace; as hereafter shall be declared in the description of the pageant. But in the opening, when her Grace understood that the Bible in English should be delivered unto her by Truth, which was therein represented by a child; she thanked the City for that gift, and said that she would oftentimes read over that book, commanding Sir John Parrat, one of he Knights which held up her canopy, to go before and to receive the book. But learning that it should be delivered unto her Grace down by a silken lace, she caused him to stay, and so passed forward. . . . And there, by appointment, the Right Worshipful Master Ranulph Cholmeley, Recorder of the City, presented to the Queen's Majesty a purse of crimson satin richly wrought with gold. . . . The Queen's Majesty, with both her hands, took the purse, and answered to him again marvelous pithily; and so pithily, that the standers by, as they embraced entirely her gracious answer, so they marvelled at the couching thereof; which was in words truly reported these:

"I thank my Lord Mayor, his Brethren, and you all. And whereas your request is that I should continue your good Lady and Queen, be ye ensured, that I will be as good unto you as ever Queen was to her people. No will in me can lack, neither do I trust shall there lack any power. And persuade yourselves, that for the safety and quietness of you all, I will not spare, if need be, to spend my blood. God thank you all."

Which answer of so noble an hearted Princess, if it moved a marvelous shout and rejoicing, it is nothing to be marvelled at, since both the heartiness thereof was so wonderful, and the words so jointly knit. . . .[5]

[5] From *The Passage of Our Most Drad Soveraigne Lady Quene Elizabeth Through the Citie of London*, in *The Progresses of Queen Elizabeth*, ed. John Nichols (London, 1823), I, 38–60.

After the events of the day before, the coronation itself was almost an anticlimax. An anonymous contemporary describes the ceremony, and the chronicler Holinshed adds a few words about the subsequent festivities.

First her Grace sat in a chair of Estate in the middle of the Church before the high altar and immediately her Grace was conducted from the said chair and led between two Lords to be proclaimed by a Bishop, Queen of England, at four places and the trumpets blowing at every proclamation. And immediately the Queen's Majesty was brought to the Chair of Estate.

And immediately her Grace was led before the high altar and there sitting a Bishop, the Queen's Majesty kneeling before the Bishop kissed the paten. Her Grace offered money and the Bishop laid it in the basin and immediately offered a pall of red silk wherein the paten was covered.

And immediately her Highness sat in a chair before the altar there being a Bishop in the pulpit preaching a sermon before the Queen's Majesty and all the Lords spiritual and temporal. And after the sermon done the Bishop bade the beads. Her Grace void out of the chair kneeling and said the Lord's Prayer.

And the Queen's Majesty being newly apparelled came before the altar and leaned upon the cushions, and over her was spread a red silken cloth. And then and there the Bishop annointed her Grace. And that done changing apparel her Grace returned and sat in her chair.

And there was a sword with a girdle put over her and upon one of her shoulders and under the other and so the sword hanging by her side. And after that two garters upon her hands, and then one crown put the Bishop upon her head, and then trumpets sounding and the Bishop put a ring upon her finger and delivered the scepter in her hand and then after, the Bishop sat a crown upon her head and the trumpets sounding. And after that her Grace offered the sword, and laid it upon the altar and returned, kneeling. And the Bishop reading upon a Book, and she having a scepter and a cross in her hand. And after that her Grace returned to the Chair of Estate.

And then the Bishop put his hand to the Queen's hand and read certain words to her Grace. And then the Lords went up to her Grace kneeling upon their knees and kissed her Grace. And after the Lords had done, the Bishops came one after another kneeling and kissing her Grace.

And after that the Bishop began the Mass, the Queen's Majesty having the scepter in the right hand and the world in the left hand, the epistle read first in Latin, and after that in English. And after that, the Bishop brought her Grace the Gospel, which also was read first in Latin and after in English, and she kissed the words of the gospel. And immediately after her Majesty went to the offering. And before her Grace was borne three naked swords, and a sword in the scabbard. And her Grace kneeling before the altar and kissed the paten, and offered certain money into the basin. And then and there was read to her Grace certain words. And then her Grace returned into her closet hearing the consecration of the Mass and her Grace kissed the pax.

And when Mass was done her Grace removed behind the high altar, and then and there her Majesty changed her apparel.

And so her Majesty was conducted from the Abbey to Westminster Hall and there dined.[6]

On Sunday the fifteenth of January her Majesty was with great solemnity crowned at Westminster, in the Abbey Church there by Doctor Oglethorp, Bishop of Carlisle. She dined in Westminster Hall, which was richly hung, and everything ordered in such royal manner as to such a regal and most solemn feast appertained. In the meantime, whilst her Grace sat at dinner, Sir Edward Dimmock, Knight, her Champion by office, came riding into the Hall in fair complete armor, mounted upon a beautiful courser, richly trapped in cloth of gold, entered the Hall, and in the midst thereof cast down his gauntlet, with offer to fight with him in her quarrel that should deny her to be the righteous and lawful Queen of this realm. The Queen, taking a cup of gold full of wine, drank to him thereof, and sent it to him for his fee, together with the cover. Now after

[6] From C. G. Bayne, ed., "The Coronation of Queen Elizabeth," *English Historical Review*, XXII (1907), 666–71. Reprinted by permission of Longmans, Green & Co. Ltd.

this, at the serving up of the wafers, the Lord Mayor of London went to the cupboard, and filling a cup of gold with hippocras, bore it to the Queen, and kneeling before her, took the assay and she receiving it of him, and drinking of it, gave the cup with the cover unto the said Lord Mayor for his fee, which cup and cover weighed sixteen ounces troy weight. Finally, this feast being celebrated with all royal ceremonies and high solemnities, due and in like cases accustomed, took end with great joy and contentation to all the beholders.[7]

[7] From Holinshed, *Chronicles,* in *The Progresses of Queen Elizabeth,* ed. John Nichols (London, 1823), I, 60–61.

3

The Queen at Court

The most characteristic setting for the Queen was her court. There in all her majesty she presided over her aristocracy; there too she conducted much of the business of government. The Queen won the devotion of her servants and courtiers through a variety of means. Undoubtedly, her most important resource was the patronage she could dispense. Titles, places, positions, financial rewards, could all be bestowed on those who performed her service. As she grew older, the courtly ceremonial grew more elaborate and her presence more commanding. Her daily performance was perfectly contrived to win respect. Yet even so, Elizabeth came to rely more and more on the device of courtly love to define—and to ease—her personal relations with the many men who flocked to court. These various tactics were generally successful; the Queen's performance won her loyal service and genuine respect from a host of men not easily given to obedience.

At court, Elizabeth was observed and described by many, foreigners as well as Englishmen. Here is an excerpt from a famous description by a German visitor, Paul Hentzner. It describes her at her zenith in 1598.

We arrived at the royal palace of Greenwich. . . . It was here Elizabeth, the present Queen, was born, and here she generally resides, particularly in summer, for the delightfulness of its situation. We were admitted . . . into the Presence-Chamber, hung with rich tapestry, and the floor after the English fashion strewed with hay, through which the Queen commonly passes on her way to chapel. At the door stood a gentleman dressed in velvet, with a gold chain, whose office was to introduce to the Queen any person of distinction that came to wait on her. It was Sunday, when there is usually the greatest attendance of Nobility. In the same hall were the Archbishop of Canterbury, the Bishop of London, a great number of Counsellors of State, officers of the Crown, and gentlemen, who waited the Queen's coming out; which she did from her own apartment, when it was time to go to prayers, attended in the following manner.

First went gentlemen, barons, earls, Knights of the Garter, all richly dressed and bare-headed; next came the Chancellor, bearing the seals in a red-silk purse, between two; one of which carried the royal scepter, the other the sword of state, in a red scabbard, studded with golden *fleurs de lis*, the point upwards. Next came the Queen in the sixty-fifth year of her age, as we were told, very majestic; her face oblong, fair, but wrinkled; her eyes small, yet black and pleasant; her nose a little hooked; her lips narrow, and her teeth black (a defect the English seem subject to, from their too great use of sugar). She had in her ears two pearls, with very rich drops; she wore false hair, and that red; upon her head she had a small crown. . . . Her bosom was uncovered, as all the English ladies have it, till they marry; and she had on a necklace of exceeding fine jewels. Her hands were small, her fingers long, and her stature neither tall nor low; her air was stately, her manner of speaking mild and obliging. That day she was dressed in white silk, bordered with pearls of the size of beans, and over it a mantle of black silk, shot with silver threads. Her train was very long, the end of it borne by a marchioness; instead of a chain, she had an oblong collar of gold and jewels. As she went along in all this state and magnificence, she spoke very graciously, first to one, then to another, whether foreign ministers, or those who attended for different reasons, in English, French, and Italian; for besides being well skilled in Greek, Latin, and the languages I have mentioned, she is mistress of Spanish, Scotch, and Dutch. Whoever speaks to her, it is kneeling; now and then she raises some with her hand. While we were there . . . a Bohemian Baron had letters to present to her; and she, after pulling off her glove, gave him her right hand to kiss, sparkling with rings and jewels, a mark of particular favor. Wherever she turned her face, as she was going along, everybody fell down on their knees. The ladies of the Court followed next to her, very handsome and well-shaped, and for the most part dressed in white. She was guarded on each side by the gentlemen pensioners, fifty in number, with gilt battle-axes. In the antechapel next to the hall where we were, petitions were presented to her, and she received them most graciously, which occasioned the acclamation of "Long live Queen Elizabeth!" She answered it with, "I thank you my good people." In the Chapel was excellent music. As soon as it, and the service was over, which scarce exceeded half an hour, the Queen returned in the same state and order, and prepared to go to dinner. . . .[1]

In rewarding her servants and courtiers, Elizabeth generally exercised a shrewd judgment. Posterity at least has found much to applaud in her frugality and caution. But to contemporaries, especially those competing for her favor, Elizabeth appeared penurious. Her carefulness was certainly useful to a monarchy in straitened financial circumstances. But liberality was still felt to be a courtly virtue. Many stories circulated about Elizabeth's carefulness. Here Francis Bacon tells two.

—Queen Elizabeth was dilatory enough in suits, of her own nature; and the Lord Treasurer Burghley, to feed her humor, would say to her, "Madam, you do well to let suitors stay; for I shall tell you, *Bis dat, qui cito dat;* If you grant them speedily, they will come again the sooner.

—Queen Elizabeth seeing Sir Edward Dyer in her garden, looked out her window and asked him in Italian, "What does a man think of when he thinks of nothing?" Sir Edward (who had not had the effect of some of the Queen's grants so soon as he had hoped and desired) paused a little and then made answer, "Madam, he thinks of a woman's promise." The Queen shrunk in her head; but was heard to say, "Well, Sir Edward, I must not confute you. Anger makes dull men witty, but it keeps them poor." [2]

[1] From Paul Hentzner, *A Journey into England in the Year MDXCIII* (Strawberry Hill, 1757), pp. 47–51.

[2] From *Apophthegms*, in *Works*, ed. James Spedding (London, 1857), VII, 174.

A similar story concerned the Queen and the poet, Edmund Spenser. Although Elizabeth provided a great theme for poetry, she did not provide much sustenance for the poets.

When her Majesty had given order that Spenser should have a reward for his poems, but Spenser could have nothing, he presented her with these verses:

It pleased your Grace upon a time
To grant me reason for my rhyme,
But from that time until this season
I heard of neither rhyme nor reason.[3]

The Elizabethan courtier was quarrelsome and unruly. One of the Queen's persistent difficulties was controlling her factious nobility. There are reports of many quarrels, sometimes violent and the Queen had to use all her tact and strength simply to keep order. Here is one example of her difficulties.

This Queen has greatly feasted Alençon's ambassador, and on one occasion when she was entertaining him at dinner she thought the sideboard was not so well furnished with pieces of plate as she would like the Frenchman to have seen it; she therefore called the Earl of Sussex, the Lord Steward, who had charge of these things, and asked him how it was there was so little plate. The Earl replied that he had, for many years, accompanied her and other sovereigns of England in their progresses, and he had never seen them take so much plate as she was carrying then. The Queen told him to hold his tongue, that he was a great rogue, and that the more good that was done to people like him the worse they got. She then turned to a certain North, who was there in the room, and asked him whether he thought there was much or little plate on the sideboard, to which he replied there was very little, and threw the

[3] From *The Diary of John Manningham*, ed. John Bruce (London, 1868), p. 43.

blame on Sussex. When North left the Queen's chamber, Sussex told him that he had spoken wrongly and falsely in what he said to the Queen, whereupon North replied that if he, Sussex, did not belong to the Council he would prove what he said to his teeth. Sussex then went to Leicester and complained of the knavish behavior of North but Leicester told him that the words he used should not be applied to such persons as North. Sussex answered that, whatever he might think of the words, North was a great knave, so that they remained offended with one another as they had been before on other matters. This may not be of importance, but I have thought well to relate it so that you may see how easily matters here may now be brought into discord if care be not taken on one side to insure support against eventualities. . . .[4]

It was part of Elizabeth's genius to discover how to manage her court despite the weakness inherent in being a woman. Her solution was to capitalize on an essentially literary convention—the device of courtly love. By transforming her courtiers into knights and herself into their lady, she could demand their service, their devotion, even their humility, without embarrassing them. That romance might flourish, Elizabeth encouraged the full panoply of courtly ceremonial, including knightly tournaments. Here is an account of an unusual event of 1580.

To these actions of arms, we may add a notable tournament on horseback, solemnized within her Majesty's palace at Westminster: which became the more rare and memorable, because it was performed in the night. The manner whereof in brief was thus.

It pleased her Majesty, according to her princely custom in the entertainment of noble strangers, to invite unto supper the Duke de Montmorency, chief Marshall of France, at that time come hither to receive the honorable Order of the Garter. This magnificent supper ended, it pleased her Highness (the weather being warm) to walk out of her chamber into the open terrace, whither also

---

[4] August 14, 1578. From *Calendar of State Papers Spanish Elizabeth* (London, 1894), pp. 606–7.

(awaiting on her) went the said Duke, and all others of the French nobility, with the ambassadors, lords and ladies of the court. At her Majesty's coming to the north side of the terrace, there were prepared and set rich chairs, cushions and carpets. In which place it pleased her to stay, entertaining most graciously the said Duke, and other noble strangers. . . .

The place with this royal preference replenished, suddenly entered Walter, Earl of Essex, and with him twelve gentlemen armed at all pieces, and well mounted. The Earl and his horse were furnished with white cloth of silver, and the rest in white satin, who after reverence done to her Majesty, marched to the east side of the court, and there in troop, stood firm. Forthwith entered Edward, Earl of Rutland, with a like number, in like sort armed and apparelled all in blue: and having presented his reverence, stayed on the west end. Before either of these bands, one chariot was drawn, and therein a fair damsel, conducted by an armed knight, who pronounced certain speeches in the French tongue, unto her Majesty. These ceremonies passed, the Queen commanded the armed men to fall unto fight: which was performed with great courage, and commendation, chiefly in the Earl of Essex, a noble personage, valorous in arms and all other ways of great virtue. Truly this action was marvelously magnificent, and appeared a sight exceeding glorious to those that were below looking upward to the terrace, where her Majesty, the lords and ladies stood, so pompously apparelled, jewelled, and furnished, as hardly can be seen the like in any Christian court, as myself saw, and other the actors (at occasions staying from fight) with great admiration did behold and think.[5]

Elizabeth's courtiers responded in the euphuistic language of love. Elizabeth became the Faerie Queene; *she also became the object of limitless flattery in her very real and earthbound court. Here is an example of a characteristic "love-letter" addressed to her, or rather, in this case, meant to be seen by her. Hundreds of others exist.*

[5] From William Segar, *Honor Military and Civill* (London, 1602), pp. 195–96.

Ralegh to Robert Cecil, July, 1592 [6]

. . . My heart was never broken till this day that I hear the Queen goes so far off, whom I have followed so many years with so great love and desire in so many journeys, and am now left behind here in a dark prison all alone. While she was yet near at hand that I might hear of her once in two or three days, my sorrows were the less, but even now my heart is cast into the depth of all misery. I that was wont to behold her riding like Alexander, hunting like Diana, walking like Venus, the gentle wind blowing her fair hair about her pure cheeks like a nymph, sometime sitting in the shade like a goddess, sometime singing like an angel, sometime playing like Orpheus; behold the sorrow of this world once amiss hath bereaved me of all. Oh! love that only shineth in misfortune, what is become of thy assurance! All wounds have scars but that of phantasy: all affections their relenting but that of woman kind. Who is the judge of friendship but adversity, or when is grace witnessed but in offenses? There were no divinity but by reason of compassion, for revenges are brutish and mortal. All those times past, the loves, the sighs, the sorrows, the desires, can they not weigh down our frail misfortune, cannot one drop of gall be hidden in so great heaps of sweetness? I may then conclude, *spes et fortuna, valete.* She is gone in whom I trusted and of me hath not one thought of mercy nor any respect of that that was. Do with me now therefore what you list. I am more weary of life than they are desirous I should perish, which if it had been for her, as it is by her, had been too happily born. . . .

[6] From *Calendar of the Manuscripts of the Marquis of Salisbury at Hatfield House* (London, 1892), IV, 220.

4
Last Years and Death

Toward the end of her reign, the Queen grew melancholy. She was old, childless, and more isolated than ever. The whole court seems to have grown somber, and there were some who grew impatient for a new reign. The Queen waited until the last to designate her successor. There are several accounts of her final days, differing in detail. All agree that her death was met by mingled regret and excitement. In the early hours of the morning, March 23, 1603, an age, as well as the life of a Queen drew to a close.

Despite her melancholy, Elizabeth's health remained good to the end. Even at 70, she danced and entertained with the spirit of a young woman.

. . . Duke Prusiano, a very courteous and brave nobleman, did resolve to come over to see England, and to come in a private way. Our ambassador in France, hearing thereof, gave notice to our secretary, who acquainting her Majesty therewith, order was taken that one should come in his company, to be a spy upon him, to know his lodgings and to discover his person. The Duke (as the fashion was) came to the court upon a Sunday, to see the Queen go to the chapel. The Queen having notice of this, and knowing him by one that stood next to him, as she came by, took some occasion to call the Lord Chamberlain, as I take it, to tie her shoe-strings, or to do some such like office; and there making a stay, she took the Duke by the hand, who followed her into the privy chamber. She did then graciously use him, and after feasted him, and gave him great entertainment . . . and then did the Queen dance a galliard very comely, and like herself, to show the vigor of her old age. He that would relate those private dancings should not have forgotten this, so famous and so well known; for even the Italians did then say that it was a wonder to see an old woman, the head of the church, being seventy years of age, to dance in that manner, and to perform her part so well. . . .[1]

In 1602, the Queen's godson, the poet John Harington, wrote to his wife describing the Queen's bad humor.

I herewith send thee, what I would God none did know, some ill bodings of the realm and its welfare. Our dear Queen, my royal godmother, and this state's natural mother, doth now bear show of human infirmity, too fast for that evil which we shall get by her death, and too slow for that good which she shall get by her releasement from pains and misery.

* * *

I find some less mindful of what they are soon to lose, than of what they may perchance hereafter get. Now, on my own part, I cannot blot from my memory's table, the goodness of our Sovereign Lady to me. . . .

It was not many days since I was bidden to her presence. I blessed the happy moment; and found her in most pitiable state. . . . Her Majesty inquired of some matters which I had written; and as she was pleased to note my fanciful brain, I was not unheedful to feed her humor, and read some verses, whereat she smiled once, and was pleased to say, "When thou dost feel creeping time at thy gate, these fooleries will please thee less; I am past my relish for such matters; thou seest my bodily meat doth not suit me well; I have eaten but one ill tasted cake since yesternight." She rated most grievously, at noon, at some who minded not to bring up certain matters of account. . . .[2]

[1] From Godfrey Goodman, in *The Court of King James I,* ed. J. S. Brewer (London, 1839), I, 17–18.

[2] December 27, 1602. From *Nugae Antiquae,* ed. Thomas Park (London, 1804), pp. 320–23.

Robert Carey describes the Queen's last days.

When I came to court, I found the Queen ill disposed and she kept her inner lodging; yet she, hearing of my arrival, sent for me. I found her in one of her withdrawing chambers, sitting low upon her cushions. She called me to her; I kissed her hand, and told her it was my chiefest happiness to see her in safety, and in health, which I wished might long continue. She took me by the hand, and wrung it hard, and said, "No, Robin, I am not well," and then discoursed with me of her indisposition, and that her heart had been sad and heavy for ten or twelve days; and in her discourse, she fetched not so few as forty or fifty great sighs. I was grieved at the first to see her in this plight; for in all my lifetime before, I never knew her fetch a sigh, but when the Queen of Scots was beheaded. . . .

I used the best words I could, to persuade her from this melancholy humor; but I found by her it was too deep-rooted in her heart, and hardly to be removed. This was upon a Saturday night, and she gave command, that the great closet should be prepared for her to go to chapel the next morning. The next day, all things being in a readiness, we long expected her coming. After eleven o'clock, one of the grooms came out, and bade make ready for the private closet, she would not go to the great. There we stayed long for her coming, but at the last she had cushions laid for her in the privy chamber hard by the closet door, and there she heard service.

From that day forwards, she grew worse and worse. She remained upon her cushions four days and nights at the least. All about her could not persuade her, either to take any sustenance, or go to bed.

I hearing that neither the physicians, nor none about her, could persuade her to take any course for her safety, feared her death would soon after ensue. I could not but think in what a wretched estate I should be left, most of my livelihood depending on her life. And hereupon I bethought myself with what grace and favor I was ever received by the King of Scots, whensoever I was sent to him. I did assure myself, it was neither unjust, nor unhonest for me to do for myself, if God, at that time, should call her to his mercy. Hereupon I wrote to the King of Scots (knowing him to be the right heir to the crown of England) and certified him in what state her Majesty was. I desired him not to stir from Edinburgh; if of that sickness she should die, I would be the first man that should bring him news of it.

The Queen grew worse and worse, because she would be so, none about her being able to persuade her to go to bed. My Lord Admiral was sent for (who, by reason of my sister's death, that was his wife, had absented himself some fortnight from court). What by fair means, what by force, he got her to bed. There was no hope of her recovery, because she refused all remedies.

On Wednesday, the 23rd of March, she grew speechless. That afternoon, by signs, she called for her council, and by putting her hand to her head, when the King of Scots was named to succeed her, they all knew he was the man she desired should reign after her.

About six at night she made signs for the Archbishop and her chaplains to come to her, at which time I went in with them, and sat upon my knees full of tears to see that heavy sight. Her Majesty lay upon her back, with one hand in the bed, and the other without. The Bishop kneeled down by her, and examined her first of her faith; and she so punctually answered all his several questions, by lifting up her eyes, and holding up her hand, as it was a comfort to all the beholders. Then the good man told her plainly what she was, and what she was to come to; and though she had been long a great Queen here upon earth, yet shortly she was to yield an account of her stewardship to the King of Kings. After this he began to pray, and all that were by did answer him. After he had continued long in prayer, till the old man's knees were weary, he blessed her, and meant to rise and leave her. The Queen made a sign with her hand. My sister, Lady Scroop, knowing her meaning, told the Bishop the Queen desired he would pray still. He did so for a long half hour after, and then thought to leave her. The second time she made sign to have him continue in prayer. He did so for half an hour more, with earnest cries to God for her soul's health, which he uttered with that fervency of spirit, as the Queen, to all our sight, much rejoiced thereat, and gave testimony, to us all of her

Christian and comfortable end. By this time it grew late, and every one departed, all but her women that attended her.

This that I heard with my ears, and did see with my eyes, I thought it my duty to set down, and to affirm it for a truth, upon the faith of a Christian; because I know there have been many false lies reported of the end and death of that good lady.

I went to my lodging, and left word with one in the cofferer's chamber to call me, if that night it was thought she would die, and gave the porter an angel to let me in at any time when I called. Between one and two of the clock on Thursday morning, he that I left in the cofferer's chamber, brought me word the Queen was dead. . . .[3]

The popular reaction to her death is described by a contemporary diarist.

This morning about three at clock her Majesty departed this life, mildly like a lamb, easily like a ripe apple from the tree. . . . Dr. Parry told me that he was present, and sent his prayers before her soul; and I doubt not but she is amongst the royal saints in Heaven in eternal joys.

About ten at clock the Counsel and divers noblemen having been a while in consultation, proclaimed James VI, King of Scots, the King of England, France, and Ireland, beginning at Whitehall gates; where Sir Robert Cecil read the proclamation which he carried in his hand, and after read again in Cheapside. Many noblemen, lords spiritual and temporal, knights, five trumpets, many heralds. The gates at Ludgate and portcullis were shut and down, by the Lord Mayor's command, who was there present, with the Aldermen, etc., and until he had a token beside promise . . . that they would proclaim the King of Scots King of England, he would not open.

Upon the death of a King or Queen in England the Lord Mayor of London is the greatest magistrate in England. All corporations and their governors continue, most of the other officers' authority

[3] From *Memoirs of the Life of Robert Carey* (London, 1759), pp. 115–23.

is expired with the prince's breath. There was a diligent watch and ward kept at every gate and street, day and night, by householders, to prevent garboils: which God be thanked were more feared than perceived.

The proclamation was heard with great expectation and silent joy, no great shouting. I think the sorrow for her Majesty's departure was so deep in many hearts they could not so suddenly show any great joy, though it could not be less than exceeding great for the succession of so worthy a king. And at night they showed it by bonfires and ringing. No tumult, no contradition, no disorder in the city; every man went about his business, as readily, as peaceably, as securely, as though there had been no change, nor any news ever heard of competitors. God be thanked, our King hath his right![4]

In a long reign, the Queen received endless compliments. But of all her admirers the most surprising may well have been the Pope himself. His praise was reluctant, but it was obviously genuine. At the time of the Armada, he told the Venetian ambassador how much he respected her.

The Pope said he had news from Spain that the Armada was ready. But the English too, are ready. "She certainly is a great Queen," he said, "and were she only a Catholic she would be our dearly beloved. Just look how well she governs; she is only a woman, only mistress of half an island, and yet she makes herself feared by Spain, by France, by the Empire, by all. She enriches her kingdom by Spanish booty, besides depriving Spain of Holland and Zeeland. . . ." He went on with pleasure to dwell on the praises and the valor of the Queen.[5]

[4] From *The Diary of John Manningham*, ed. John Bruce (London, 1868), pp. 146–47.
[5] From *Calendar of State Papers Venetian* (London, 1894), VIII, 345–46.

PART TWO

ELIZABETH I LOOKS AT THE WORLD

5

The Queen's Servants

All the sixteenth-century political manuals agreed that the first condition of successful rule was to find wise and capable men to counsel and assist the monarch. And here Elizabeth excelled. To find able men and to keep them loyal and subordinate was not easy for a young woman in a masculine and unruly age. But Elizabeth had the insight and found the means to discover and hold servants remarkable for their devotion and ability, men like William Cecil, Francis Walsingham, and Thomas Smith. At court she kept the parties divided and dependent upon her. A successful balance between interests and temperaments allowed her to retain her independence and to secure the best advice from all points of view. In this light we may view the long rivalry between William Cecil and Robert Dudley. In the last years of her reign, however, one generation of courtiers was replaced by another. New men, young, vigorous and often impatient of the aging Queen, raised a fresh challenge to her rule. For the most part she weathered it with the old methods, combining charm and imperiousness with the balancing of factions. Only the Earl of Essex remained recalcitrant and in the end openly rebellious. But the Queen was far too firmly seated on the throne to be undone by that talented but erratic young man.

Needless to say, each of the Queen's relationships with her servants is a long and fascinating story, too long to recount simply. To complicate matters, each relationship existed not only between Queen and servant, but between man and woman. Undoubtedly, Elizabeth's affections were often stirred by her courtiers; Robert Dudley is the most obvious example. How far then, were her actions governed by policy, how far by the emotions of a woman? Surely it is through these relationships that we approach closest to the person behind the throne. Yet Elizabeth remains enigmatic, revealing her inner self very little and then only in flashes. For whatever stirred her woman's heart, she remained always—and first—the Queen of England, forever concealing her personal life behind her public character.

The documents that follow illustrate something of the character of these relationships, concentrating on a few of her leading servants and courtiers.

LEICESTER

For many years two men Robert Dudley and William Cecil, seemed to dominate and to divide Elizabeth's Council. They were as unlike as rivals could be. Dudley was about the same age as Elizabeth, masculine and attractive. For a time it seemed at though Elizabeth would marry him, but the apparent murder of his wife, Amy Robsart, in 1560, caused a scandal that made the match unwise. Rumors soon spread abroad. Catherine de Medici was heard to mock the possibility of a match between Elizabeth and "her horse-keeper," a reference to Dudley's position as Master of the Horse. The Queen put on a brave face, but the likelihood of marriage had receded. Here is an account of the reaction of Elizabeth to the news from France.

. . . The 27th, I spake with her Majesty at Greenwich. . . . When I came to the point that touched [Dudley] . . . which I set forth in as vehement terms as the case required . . . she laughed, and forthwith turned herself to the one side and to the other, and set her hand upon her face. She thereupon told me, that the matter [the alleged murder] had been tried in the country and found to be contrary to that which was reported, saying that he [Dudley] was then in the Court, and none of his at the attempt at his wife's house; and that it fell out as should neither touch his honesty nor her honor. . . .

. . . The Queen's Majesty looketh not so hearty and well as she did . . . and surely the matter of my Lord Robert doth much perplex her, and it [the marriage] is never like to take place, and the talk thereof is somewhat slack, as generally misliked. . . .[1]

Leicester did not give up easily however and the Queen—either for political purposes or because she continued to love him—kept the prospect of marriage alive. Here the Spanish ambassador reports (January 31, 1562).

My last letters were written on the 10th and 17th instant, and since then Lord Robert has intimated to me and has caused others to tell me, that he is desirous that your Majesty should write to the Queen in his favor, and persuading her to marry him. He would like this boon to be obtained for him without writing himself to your Majesty, as he fears the answer might make conditions with regard to religion which were out of his power. . . . And as I had an opportunity afterwards of speaking to the Queen on the matter, I asked her what was the meaning of Lord Robert's request after they had both been so convinced of your Majesty's goodwill towards the marriage. She said she was as free from any engagement to marry as the day she was born, notwithstanding what the world might think or say, but that she had quite made up her mind to marry nobody whom she had not seen or known, and consequently she might be obliged to marry in England, in which case she could find no person more fitting than Lord Robert. She would be glad that all friendly princes should write in his favor and particularly your Majesty, who might take advantage of what the world was saying about the marriage, and write advising her thereto, so that if she should feel disposed to it, people might not say that she had married to satisfy her own desires, but rather by the advice of her princely friends and relatives. This, she said, was what Robert

[1] Nicholas Jones to Nicholas Throckmorton in *Hardwicke State Papers* (London, 1778), pp. 166–67.

wanted—as for her, she asked for nothing—but she did not see that your Majesty risked anything by doing as Robert requested, even though the marriage did not take place. At last, seeing that I did not promise what was asked, she said there was no necessity for it, only for appearance sake, and in any case the marriage could be effected when she decided, without your Majesty's letter, although, to speak plainly, if it were to take place without your Majesty's favor, Lord Robert would have little cause to feel obliged or bound to your Majesty. . . .[2]

Leicester's fortunes rose and fell with those of Elizabeth's other suitors. He also had difficulties with rivals at Court. But rumors of marriage persisted and the Queen did nothing to quash them. In 1566, the Venetian ambassador reported the following story.

It being the custom in England on the day of the Epiphany to name a King, a gentleman was chosen who had lately found favor with Queen Elizabeth, and a game of questions and answers being proposed, as usual amongst merry-makers, he commanded Lord Robert to ask the Queen, who was present, which was the most difficult to erase from the mind, an evil opinion created by a wicked informer, or jealousy? And Lord Robert, being unable to refuse, obeyed. The Queen replied courteously that both things were difficult to get rid of, but that, in her opinion, it was much more difficult to remove jealousy.

The game being ended, Lord Robert, angry with that gentleman for having put this question to the Queen, and assigning perhaps a sense to this proceeding other than jest, sent to threaten him, through the medium of a friend, that he would castigate him with a stick. The gentleman replied that this was not punishment for equals, and that if Lord Robert came to insult him, he would find whether his sword cut and thrust, and that if Lord Robert had no quarrel with him Lord Robert was to let him know where he was to be found, because he would then go to Lord Robert quite alone;

[2] From *Calendar of State Papers Spanish Elizabeth* (London, 1892), I, 224–25.

but the only answer Lord Robert gave was that this gentleman was not his equal, and that he would postpone chastising him till he thought it time to do so.

Shortly afterwards the gentleman went to the Queen, and let her know the whole circumstance. Her Majesty was very angry with Lord Robert, and said that if by her favor he had become insolent he should soon reform, and that she would lower him just as she had at first raised him; and she banished from the Court the gentleman who had taken his message. Lord Robert was quite confused by the Queen's anger, and, placing himself in one of the rooms of the palace in deep melancholy, remained there four consecutive days, and showing by his despair that he could no longer live; so the Queen, moved to pity, restored him again to her favor; yet, as the Ambassador told me, his good fortune, if perhaps not impeded, will at least have been delayed a little, for it had been said that she would shortly proclaim him Duke and marry him.[3]

> *Affection lingered long after the prospect of marriage had faded. In 1585 Leicester was given command of an expedition to the Low Countries. But he soon offended Elizabeth (who wished to keep her intervention there discreet) by accepting the title of Governor. Elizabeth's reprimand displays her at her most imperious.*

How contemptuously we conceive ourself to have been used by you, you shall by this bearer understand, whom we have expressly sent unto you to charge you withal. We could never have imagined, had we not seen it fall out in experience, that a man raised up by ourself, and extraordinarily favored by us above any other subject of this land, would have in so contemptible a sort broken our commandment, in a cause that so greatly toucheth us in honor; whereof, although you have showed yourself to make but little account, in most undutiful a sort, you may not therefore think that we have so little care of the reparation thereof as we mind to pass so great a wrong in silence unredressed: and, therefore, our express pleasure and commandment is, that, all delays and excuses laid

[3] From *Calendar of State Papers Venetian* (London, 1890), **VII**, 374–75.

apart, you do presently, upon the duty of your allegiance, obey and fulfill whatsoever the bearer hereof shall direct you to do in our name: whereof fail you not, as you will answer the contrary at your uttermost peril.[4]

Leicester was recalled; Camden reports his successful encounter with the Queen in which, as always, he weathered the storm. It was his last; a year later the earl was dead.

Leicester being returned, and smelling that there was an accusation framed against him by Buckhurst and others for ill managing of affairs in Holland, and that he was to be summoned before the Council, cast himself down privately at the Queen's feet, and with tears craved her protection; beseeching her, that whom she had sent forth with honor at his first departure, she would not now receive with disgrace at his return; and whom she had raised up from the ground, she would not now bring alive to his grave. And with such flattering speeches he so mollified the Queen's offended mind, that her noble displeasure abated, and she received him into former grace and favor. Insomuch as when he was expected the next day to come to his answer, he took his place in the Council, and did not kneel at the upper end of the table, as the manner is; and when the Secretary began to read the heads of his accusation, he interrupted him, complaining that he was injuriously dealt withal in his absence, for that his public commission was restrained by private instructions: and so appealing to the Queen, he avoided the whole weight of the accusation, not without the secret chafing and indignation of his adversaries.[5]

BURGHLEY

Elizabeth's friendship with William Cecil began early; she corresponded with him from 1548. Upon becoming Queen,

[4] From *Correspondence of Robert Dudley . . . 1585–86*, ed. J. Bruce (London, 1844), p. 110.

[5] From William Camden, *The History of Elizabeth*, 3rd ed. (London, 1675), p. 400.

she adopted him as her most valued servant, making him Secretary of State (1558), Baron Burghley (1571), and Lord High Treasurer (1572). Cecil was never a courtier. He was rather a tireless civil servant; ambitious, but devoted and immensely capable. His relationship with the Queen was not always smooth. Rivalry with Leicester was one source of anxiety; occasional differences of policy was another. But with age, the Queen grew more attached to Cecil and more dependent on his judgment.

Immediately upon her accession she admitted him to her Privy Council with the following injunction.

I give you this charge, that you shall be my Privy Counsellor, and content yourself to take pains for me and my realm. This judgment I have of you, that you will not be corrupted with any manner of gifts, and that you will be faithful to the state, and that, without respect of my private will, you will give me that counsel that you think best: and if you shall know anything necessary to be declared to me of secrecy, you shall show it to myself only, and assure yourself I will not fail to keep taciturnity therein. And therefore herewith I charge you.[6]

Sir Thomas Smith's letter reveals the Queen's growing dependence on Cecil.

My very good Lord, your hasty going hence hath made, as appeareth, all things to turn backward. I had somewhat ado to get to the Queen, and more to get anything signed.

I would have had her Majesty sign Mr. Dale's dispatch straight, saying it was ready, and have kept it still, or left it with me, until her Highness thought good to send him. It would not be; and I perceive until that your Lordship come again, there will be no good done. I said there were other things to be done, beside all these

[6] From Harington, in *Nugae Antiquae,* ed. Thomas Park (London, 1804), pp. 68–69.

instructions. . . . But I perceive until you return, nothing will be done. . . .[7]

The Queen's affection grew accordingly. Here she writes to Cecil fondly.

Sir Spirit, I doubt I do nickname you, for those of your kind (they say) have no sense, but I have of late seen an *ecce signum*, that if an ass kick you, you feel it too soon. I will recant you from being my spirit, if ever I perceive that you disdain not such a feeling. Serve God, fear the King, and be a good fellow to the rest. Let never care appear in you for such a rumor, but let them well know, that you rather desire the righting of such wrongs, by making known their error, then you to be so silly a soul, as to foreslow that you ought to do, or not freely deliver what you think meetest, and pass of no man so much, as not to regard her trust, who puts it in you.

God bless you and long may you last.[8]

Until his death in 1598, Cecil continued to serve Elizabeth, after the fashion indicated in a letter of advice he wrote to his son, and successor, Robert.

I do hold, and will always, this course in such matters as I differ in opinion from her Majesty. As long as I may be allowed to give advice I will not change my opinion by affirming the contrary. For that were to offend God to whom I am sworn first. But as a servant I will obey her Majesty's commandment and no wise contrary the same. Presuming that she being God's chief minister here, it shall be God's will to have her commandment obeyed;

[7] January 7, 1572. From *Queen Elizabeth and Her Times,* ed. Thomas Wright (London, 1838), I, 448.

[8] May 5, 1583. From *Queen Elizabeth and Her Times,* ed. Thomas Wright (London, 1838), II, 201.

after that I have performed my duty as a counselor and shall in my heart, with her commandments to have such good successes as I am sure she intendeth.

You see I am in a mixture of divinity and policy. Preferring in policy her Majesty above all others on the earth and in divinity the King of Heaven above all betwixt Alpha and Omega.

These my cogitations you may use to your own good. God bless you. Your loving father.[9]

A last anecdote, told by Francis Bacon, shows the Queen, as always, affirming her independent authority, on this occasion in a matter of patronage.

Queen Elizabeth was entertained by my Lord Burghley at Theobalds and at her going away, my Lord obtained of the Queen to make seven knights. . . . They were placed in a rank, as the Queen should pass by the hall; and to win antiquity of knighthood, in order, as my Lord favored; though indeed the more principal gentlemen were placed lowest. The Queen was told of it, and said nothing; but when she went along, she passed them all by, as far as the screen, as if she had forgot it: and when she came to the screen, she seemed to take herself with the manner, and said, "I had almost forgot what I promised." With that she turned back, and knighted of the lowest first, and so upward. Whereupon Mr. Stanhope, of the privy-chamber, a while after told her: "Your Majesty was too fine for my Lord Burghley." She answered, "I have but fulfilled the scripture; the first shall be last, and the last first."[10]

RALEGH

In the last years of Elizabeth's reign, new young men rose swiftly to prominence. Among them was Walter Ralegh. This famous tale—probably apocryphal—illustrates the romance

[9] March 13, 1596. From *Desiderata Curiosa*, ed. Francis Peck (London, 1732), I, 10.

[10] From *Apophthegms*, in *Works*, ed. James Spedding (London, 1857), VII, 157–58.

*that surrounded the Queen and that she deliberately culti-
vated.*

[Ralegh] coming to court, found some hopes of the Queen's
favors reflecting upon him. This made him write in a glass window,
obvious to the Queen's eye,

Fain would I climb, yet fear I to fall.

Her Majesty, either espying or being shown it, did under write,

If thy heart fails thee, climb not at all.

However, he at last climbed up by the stairs of his own desert.
But his introduction into the court bore an elder date from this
occasion. The Captain Ralegh coming out of Ireland to the English
court in good habit (his clothes being then a considerable part of
his estate) found the Queen walking, till, meeting with a plashy
place, she seemed to scruple going thereon. Presently, Ralegh cast
and spread his new plush cloak on the ground; whereon the Queen
trod gently, rewarding him afterward with many suits, for his so
free and seasonable tender of so fair a foot-cloth. Thus an adven-
tageous admission into the first notice of a prince is more than
half a degree to preferment.[11]

THE EARL OF ESSEX

*Of the new men at court, first easily was the impetuous
young Robert, Earl of Essex. Handsome and well-born—his
stepfather was Leicester, his mother a cousin of Elizabeth's—
he rose swiftly to prominence. The Queen alternately encouraged him and resisted his brash efforts to secure more and
more influence. What she would have liked no doubt was to
repeat the nice balance she had kept so long between Leicester
and Burghley, this time between Essex and Robert Cecil. But
Essex was no Leicester; his ambition and pride were not
accompanied by the cunning of his model, and were destined,
as in an Elizabethan tragedy, to lead to his downfall.*

---

[11] From Thomas Fuller, *Worthies of England* (London, 1840), I, 419.

Essex became a favorite at court at the age of 20, receiving Leicester's old position of Master of the Horse (1587). He was soon quarreling with several other young courtiers, but especially Ralegh. He also quarreled with the Queen. On one occasion he defied her orders to remain at court and set sail in 1589 for adventures against Spain. Her reprimand here was soon forgotten, however.

Your sudden and undutiful departure from our presence and your place of attendance, you may easily conceive how offensive it is, and ought to be, unto us. Our great favors bestowed on you without deserts, hath drawn you thus to neglect and forget your duty; for other constructions we cannot make of these your strange actions. Not meaning, therefore, to tolerate this your disordered part, we gave directions to some of our Privy Council to let you know our express pleasure for your immediate repair hither; which you have not performed, as your duty doth bind you, increasing greatly thereby your former offence and undutiful behaviour, in departing in such sort without our privity, having so special office of attendance and charge near our person. We do therefore charge and command you forthwith upon receipt of these our letters, all excuses and delays set apart, to make your present and immediate repair unto us, to understand our farther pleasure. Whereof see you fail not, as you will be loath to incur our indignation, and will answer for the contrary at your uttermost peril.[12]

Elizabeth's advice to Essex (here reported by Anthony Bacon) was sincerely meant, and as long as he followed it, he was treated with unexampled generosity.

Yesternight it pleased the Queen's Majesty to use most gracious words unto him, to wit, that his desire to be in action, and to give farther proof of this valor and prowess was to be liked and highly commended; but that she loved him and her realm too much to

---

[12] From Walter Devereux, *Lives and Letters of the Earls of Essex* (London, 1853), I, 204–5.

hazard his person in any lesser action than that, which should import her crown and state: and therefore willed him to be content, and gave him a warrant of 4,000 pounds sterling, saying, "Look to thyself, good Essex, and be wise to help thyself, without giving thy enemies advantage; and my hand shall be readier to help thee than any other." [13]

In 1593 Essex was admitted to the Privy Council. Here began a great contest for influence with that other rising star, Robert Cecil. With characteristic abandon, Essex began to press the Queen for favors. Particularly, he sought preferment for his followers. But their advancement threatened the precarious balance by which Elizabeth insured her rule. When therefore Essex sought office for Francis Bacon, the Queen resisted. She may have had more than one motive. Bacon had unwisely offended Elizabeth by speaking against a subsidy in Parliament. And too, his obvious brilliance was lodged in an equivocal character not likely to appeal to the Queen. But her resistance to Essex was no doubt the main issue. Here Essex reports one of his many rebuffs to Bacon.

I have received your letter, and since I have had opportunity to deal freely with the Queen. I have dealt confidently with her, as of a matter wherein I did more labor to overcome her delays than that I did fear her denial. I told her how much you were thrown down with the correction she had already given you; that she might in that point hold herself already satisfied. And because I found that Tanfield had been most propounded to her, I did most disable him. I find the Queen very reserved, staying herself from giving any kind of hope, yet not passionate against you till I grew passionate for you. Then she said that none thought you fit for the place but my Lord Treasurer and myself; marry the others must some of them say [so] before us for fear or for flattery. I told her the most and wisest of her Council had delivered their opinions, and preferred you before all men for that place. And if it would please her

---

[13] Anthony Bacon to Francis Bacon, July 26, 1594, in *Memoirs of the Reign of Queen Elizabeth,* ed. Thomas Birch (London, 1744), I, 181.

Majesty to think that whatsoever they said contrary to their own words when they spake without witness, might be as factiously spoken as the other way flatteringly, she should not be deceived. Yet if they had been never for you, but contrarily against you, I thought my credit, joined with the approbation and mediation of her greatest counsellors, might prevail in a greater matter than this; and urged her that though she could not signify her mind to others, I might have a secret promise; wherein I should receive great comfort, as in the contrary great unkindness. She said she neither was persuaded nor would hear of it till Easter, when she might advise with her Council, who were now all absent; and therefore in passion bade me go to bed, if I would talk of nothing else. Wherefore in passion I went away, saying while I was with her I could not but solicit for the cause and the man I so much affected, and therefore I would retire myself till I might be more graciously heard. And so we parted. . . .[14]

Essex at least gained his opportunity for adventure in a bold expedition against Cadiz in 1596. The Queen had to be cajoled and persuaded to release him but finally relented and sent him off with a prayer. Cadiz was a great success and Essex's reputation with the people was established. His quarrels with the Queen continued, however, although each rapprochement brought him new rewards, among them Earl Marshall (1597) and Chancellor of Cambridge University (1598). In 1598, Elizabeth confronted again the question of war or peace. Camden recounts her divided councils—Essex for war, Burghley for peace—and the Queen's confrontation with Essex.

Burghley Lord Treasurer, for the consideration aforesaid, and the advantages of peace, which are certain, profitable and necessary, inclined to peace, knowing the chance of war to be uncertain, the charges infinite, the treasure of England exhausted, the nature of the common people of England inclinable to sedition, if they be oppressed with extraordinary payments, that there was an inbred

[14] April 26, 1594. From *The Letters and the Life of Francis Bacon,* ed. James Spedding (London, 1861), I, 289.

disaffection in the vulgar towards the nobility, small hope of assistance from the estates, our neighbors round about to be suspected, many treacherous at home, and the Spaniard's treasure not to be drawn dry: and (as he said) no good could come to England by this war, but only an aversion of evil, which amongst good things is reputed the least.

Essex argued to the contrary, and having been bred up to a military life, and got great renown, by no means would assent to a peace; but by reasons drawn from the subtle natures and dispositions of the Spaniards, their insatiate desire of enlarging their empire, their inveterate hatred against England and the Queen, their diversity of religion from ours, the Bishop of Rome's power in dispensing, that axiom, *That faith is not to be kept with heretics,* an anxious suspicion and fear of future dangers, and such other like matters, which I have already related, stiffly maintained, that no peace could be made with the Spaniards but such as would be dishonorable, and fraudulent on their side: insomuch as the Lord Treasurer said that he breathed forth nothing but war, slaughter, and blood; and after a hot dispute about this matter, as if he presaged what would after be, he drew forth a psalm-book, and saying nothing, pointed him to this verse, *Men of blood shall not live out half their days.* . . .

Concerning this business of the peace, and the choosing of some meet and able person to look after the affairs of Ireland, there grew a smart debate between the Queen and Essex, none else being present but the Lord Admiral, Sir Robert Cecil Secretary, and Windebank Clerk of the Signet. For whereas she thought Sir William Knolles, Uncle to Essex, the fittest man of any to be sent over into Ireland, and Essex obstinately insisted that Sir George Carew was a fitter person than he, on purpose to rid the court of him, yet could not by all his persuasions draw her to it; quite forgetting himself, and neglecting his duty, he uncivilly turned his back upon her as it were in contempt, and gave her a scornful look. She, not enduring such behavior, gave him a box on the ear, and bade him get him gone and be hanged. He presently laid his hand on his sword; and the Lord Admiral stepping between, he sware a great oath, that he neither could nor would put up so great an affront and indignity, neither would he have taken it at King

Henry VIII's hands; and in a great passion withdrew himself presently from the Court. . . . Yet within a little while, after he became more submissive, obtained his pardon, and was received again by her into favor, who always thought it less mis-beseeming to offend and anger a man than to hate him. Yet hereupon his friends began shrewdly to fear his ruin, who had observed that fortune is seldom reconciled to her foster-children whom she hath once forsaken; and princes more seldom to those whom they before offended.[15]

> *Essex was undone in Ireland. He sought to lead the expedition there to suppress the rebellion of Tyrone but against the advice of Bacon and the inclination of the Queen. And indeed, Ireland was an unrelieved disaster, a series of vacillations and defeats that were extremely costly. Essex began badly by choosing Christopher Blount as his deputy and then creating large numbers of knights; both against Elizabeth's express command. He ended worse by concluding his grand expedition with a truce rather than a victory. By then the Queen's patience was exhausted. In September, 1599, Essex panicked and rushed home, leaving his army abroad. Here John Harington, who had been with Essex, describes the Queen's anger.*

. . . On the Lord Deputy's coming home, when I did come into her presence; she chafed much, walked fastly to and fro, looked with discomposure in her visage; and, I remember, she catched my girdle when I kneeled to her, and swore, "By God's son I am no Queen; that man is above me;—Who gave him command to come here so soon? I did send him on other business." It was long before more gracious discourse did fall to my hearing; but I was then put out of my trouble, and bid, "Go home." I did not stay to be bidden twice; if all the Irish rebels had been at my heels, I should not have had better speed, for I did now flee from one whom I both loved and feared too.[16]

[15] From William Camden, *The History of Elizabeth*, 3rd ed. (London, 1675), pp. 555–56.
[16] From *Nugae Antiquae*, ed. Thomas Park (London, 1804), p. 356.

6

The Queen and the People

Elizabeth understood at once the importance of popular support. Immediately, upon her accession, she began to court her people. With exquisite tact she turned every opportunity to account. And she made endless occasions by her many progresses through the countryside. The documents below show her charming the citizens of London, the scholars at Cambridge, and the townspeople of Warwick. But the climax of her popularity was probably reached in the crisis of the Armada. Her address to the army at Tilbury is characteristic. The nation rallied around its monarch, and the triumph of England over Spain proclaimed Elizabeth's glory to the world.

This ballad by William Birch is in the form of a dialogue between Elizabeth and England. It was written shortly after her accession. (The missing verses recount Elizabeth's misadventures under Mary.)

England: Come over the born Bessy
    Come over the born Bessy
    Sweet Bessy come over to me;
    And I shall thee take,
    And my dear Lady make
    Before all other that ever I see.

 Bessy: Me think I hear a voice,
    At whom I do rejoice,
    And answer thee now I shall:—
    Tell me, I say,
    What art thou that bids me come away,
    And so earnestly dost me call?

  E: I am thy lover fair,

Hath chose thee to mine heir,
And my name is merry England;
Therefore, come away,
And make no more delay,
Sweet Bessy! give me thy hand.

B: Here is my hand,
My dear lover England,
I am thine both with mind and heart,
Forever to endure,
Thou mayest be sure,
Until death us two do part.

E: Lady, this long space
Have I loved thy grace,
More than I durst well say;
Hoping, at the last,
When all storms were past,
For to see this joyful day.

B: Yet my lover, England,
Ye shall understand
How fortune on me did lower:
I was tumbled and tossed
From pillar to post,
And prisoner in the Tower.

E: Why, dear Lady, I trow,
Those madmen did not know,
That ye were daughter unto King Harry;
And a princess of birth,
One of the noblest on earth
And sister unto Queen Mary.

B: Yes:—yet I must forgive
All such as do live,
If they will hereafter amend;
And for those that are gone,
God forgive them every one,
And his mercy on them extend!

*   *   *

E: Dear Lady and Queen,
I trust it shall be seen,

Ye shall reign quietly without strife;
And if any traitors there be,
Of any kind or degree,
I pray God send them short life.

B: I trust all faithful hearts
Will play true subjects' parts,
Knowing me their Queen, and true heir by right:
And that much the rather,
For the love of my father,
That worthy prince, King Henry th'eight.

E: Therefore, let us pray
To God, both night and day,
Continually and never to cease,
That he will preserve your grace,
To reign over us long space,
In tranquility, wealth, and peace.

Both: All honor, laud, and praise,
Be to the Lord God, always,
Who hath all princes' hearts in his hands;
That by his power and might
He may guide them aright,
For the wealth of all Christian lands.[1]

Elizabeth's personal vanity was proverbial. But her care for her appearance had a practical character as well. She was intent on shaping her own public image and left nothing to chance. Here are some recollections by Nicholas Hilliard, the great miniaturist.

This makes me remember the words also and reasoning of her Majesty when first I came in her Highness' presence to draw, who after showing me how she noted great difference of shadowing in the works and diversity of drawers of sundry nations, and that the Italians [who] had the name to be the cunningest and to draw best, shadowed not, requiring of me the reason of it, seeing that best to show one-self needeth no shadow of place but rather the open

---

[1] From *The Harleian Miscellany*, ed. Thomas Park (London, 1813), X, 260–62.

light; to which I granted [and] affirmed that shadows in pictures were indeed caused by the shadow of the place or coming in of the light as only one way into the place at some small or high window, which many workmen covet to work in for ease to their sight, and to give unto them a grosser line and a more apparent line to be discerned and maketh the work emboss well, and show very well afar off, which to limning work needeth not, because it is to be viewed of necessity in hand near unto the eye. Here her Majesty conceived the reason, and therefore chose her place to sit in for that purpose in the open alley of a goodly garden, where no tree was near, nor any shadow at all, save that as the heaven is lighter than the earth so must that little shadow that was from the earth. This her Majesty's curious demand hath greatly bettered my judgment, besides divers other like questions in art by her most excellent Majesty, which to speak or write of were fitter for some better clerk.[2]

Here are some examples of the Queen's progresses. In the first, the Spanish ambassador, Guzman de Silva, reports in 1568.

The Queen arrived in this city on the 6th in good health and continued her progress which as I have said, will only be in the neighborhood, as she is careful to keep near at hand when troubles and disturbances exist in adjacent counties. She came by the river as far as Reading, and thence through the country in a carriage, open on all sides, that she might be seen by the people, who flocked all along the roads as far as the Duke of Norfolk's houses where she alighted. She was received everywhere with great acclamations and signs of joy, as is customary in this country; whereat she was extremely pleased and told me so, giving me to understand how beloved she was by her subjects and how highly she esteemed this, together with the fact that they were peaceful and contented

[2] From *A Treatise Concerning the Arte of Limning,* ed. P. Norman (Oxford, 1911–1912), I, 28–29.

whilst her neighbors on all sides are in such trouble. She attributed it all to God's miraculous goodness. She ordered her carriage to be taken sometimes where the crowd seemed thickest and stood up and thanked the people. . . .[3]

In 1572, the Queen visited Warwick.

This oration ended, Robert Philips, Bailiff, rising out of the place where he kneeled, approached near to the coach or chariot wherein her Majesty sat; and coming to the side thereof, kneeling down, offered unto her Majesty a purse very fair wrought, and in the purse twenty pounds, all in sovereigns; which her Majesty putting forth her hand received, showing withal a very benign and gracious countenance, and, smiling, said to the Earl of Leicester, "My Lord, this is contrary to your promise!"

And, turning towards the Bailiff, Recorder, and Burgesses, said, "Bailiff, I thank you, and you all, with all my heart, for your good wills; and I am very loath to take anything at your hands now, because you at the last time of my being here presented us to our great liking and contentation; and it is not the manner to be always presented with gifts: and I am the more unwilling to take anything of you, because I know that a mite of their hands is as much as a thousand pounds of some others. Nevertheless, because you shall not think that I mislike of your good wills, I accept it with most hearty thanks to you all; praying God that I may perform, as Mr. Recorder saith, such benefit as is hoped."

And therewithal offered her hand to the Bailiff to kiss, who kissed it; and then she delivered to him again his mace, which before the oration he had delivered to her Majesty, which she kept in her lap all the time of the oration. And after the mace delivered, she called Mr. Aglionby to her, and offered her hand to him to kiss, withal smiling, said, "Come hither, little Recorder. It was told me that you would be afraid to look upon me, or to speak boldly; but you were not so afraid of me as I was of you; and I now thank

[3] From *Calendar of State Papers Spanish Elizabeth* (London, 1894), II, 50–51.

you for putting me in mind of my duty, and that should be in me."

And so thereupon showing a most gracious and favorable countenance to all the Burgesses and company, said again, "I most heartily thank you all, my good people." [4]

London was the very center of Elizabeth's popularity. Bishop Goodman recalls the year of the Armada.

In the year '88, I did then live at the upper end of the Strand near St. Clement's Church, when suddenly there came a report unto us (it was in December, much about five of the clock at night, very dark) that the Queen was gone to council, and if you will see the Queen you must come quickly. Then we all ran; when the Court gates were set open, and no man did hinder us from coming in. There we came where there was a far greater company than was usually at Lenten sermons; and when we had stayed there an hour and that the yard was full, there being a number of torches, the Queen came out in great state. Then we cried, "God save your Majesty! God save your Majesty!" Then the Queen turned unto us and said, "God bless you all, my good people!" Then we cried again, "God save your Majesty! God save your Majesty!" Then the Queen said again unto us, "You may well have a greater prince, but you shall never have a more loving prince:" and so looking one upon another awhile the Queen departed. This wrought such an impression upon us, for shows and pageants are ever best seen by torchlight, that all the way long we did nothing but talk what an admirable Queen she was, and how we would adventure our lives to do her service.[5]

The Queen visited the two universities on several occasions. As often, her visits were proclaimed in published accounts. Here are some extracts from The Triumphs of the Muses; or

[4] From *The Progresses of Queen Elizabeth*, ed. John Nichols (London, 1823), I, 315–16.

[5] From *The Court of King James I*, ed. J. S. Brewer (London, 1839), p. 163.

the grand Reception and Entertainment of Queen Elizabeth at
Cambridge 1564.

[*Elizabeth arrived on August 5 and attended services.*] Which
being ended, the Queen's Majesty came forth of her traverse, and
went toward the lodging by the privy way. . . . And as she went,
she thanked God that had sent her to this University, where she,
altogether against her expectation, was so received, that she thought,
she could not be better.

[*On Sunday she witnessed a play by Plautus and heard a sermon,
by Andrew Perne.*] About the midst of his sermon, her Majesty
sent the Lord Hunsdon to will him, to put on his cap: which he did
unto the end. At which time, or he could get out of the pulpit, by
the Lord Chamberlain sent him word, it was the first sermon that
ever she heard in Latin and she thought she would never hear a
better.

[*The Queen then listened to some disputations but time ran out
on Dr. Baker the Vice Chancellor. However*] . . . she willed him
to dispute also, alleging in open audience, that he was her host and
she feared to lack her lodging, if she should chance to come again
hereafter if he should be disappointed.

At the end thereof [of the disputations] the Lords, and especially
the Duke of Norfolk and the Lord Robert [Dudley] kneeling
down, humbly desired her Majesty to speak somewhat to the University and in Latin. Her Highness at the first refused, saying, that
if she might speak her mind in English she would not stick at the
matter. But (understanding by Mr. Secretary [Cecil]) that nothing
might be said openly to the University in English, she required
him the rather to speak because he was Chancellor and the Chancellor is the Queen's mouth. Whereunto he answered, that he was
Chancellor of the University and not hers.

Then the Bishop of Ely kneeling said that three words of her
mouth were enough. So being moved on every side, she spake at
length as followeth.

"Although that womanly shamefacedness, most celebrated University and most faithful subjects, might well determine me from

delivering this my unlabored speech and oration before so great an assembly of the learned; yet the intercession of my nobles and my own good-will towards the University, have prevailed with me to say something.

"And I am persuaded to this thing by two motives.

"The first is, the increase of good letters; which, I much desire, and with the most earnest wishes, pray for. The other is, as I hear, all your expectations.

"As to the increase of good letters, I remember that passage in Demosthenes, 'The words of superiors have the weight of books with their inferiors; and the sayings of princes retain the authority of laws with their subjects.' This one thing then I would have you all remember, that there will be no directer, no fitter course, either to make your fortunes, or to procure the favor of your Prince, than, as you have begun, to ply your studies diligently. Which that you would do, I beg and beseech you all.

"As to the other motive, to wit your expectations; I only say, that there is nothing I should rather have chose to have let alone than this one thing. Because your benevolent minds, I perceive, entertain so high thoughts of me.

"And now I come to the University. This morning I have beheld your sumptuous edifices, erected by several most illustrious princes, my ancestors, for the sake of learning. And, in seeing them a grief seized me and those anxieties of mind which are said once to have caught hold of Alexander the Great; who, when he had perused the many monuments of other princes, turning to his favorite or rather counsellor, much lamented, that there should ever have lived any who out-went him either in time or actions. So no less did I grieve, when I beheld your structures, that I as yet had done nothing of this sort.

"The common proverb, which though it cannot utterly remove my concern, may yet assuage it; hath nevertheless a little comforted me. The saying I mean is, 'Rome was not built in a day.'

"For my age is not yet so far advanced, nor again is it already so long since I began to reign, but that, before I pay my last debt to nature (if cruel Atropos do not too soon cut the thread of my life) I may erect some passing good work. And from this design, as long as I have any life left, I shall never depart. And if it should happen (which indeed I cannot tell how soon it may) that I must die, before I can complete this thing, which I now assure; yet will I leave some famous monument behind me, whereby both my memory shall be renowned, and I, by my example, may excite others to the like worthy actions; and also make you all more ready to pursue your studies.

"But now you see the difference between true learning, and an education not well retained. Of the one of which you yourselves are all more than sufficient evidence; and of the other I, too inconsiderately indeed, have made you all witnesses.

"It is time then that your ears, which have been so long detained by this barbarous sort of an oration, should now be released from the pain of it."

At this, all marvelously astonished and inwardly revising, spoke forth in open voice, "Vivat Regina!" But the Queen's Majesty said on the other side, in respect of her oration, "Taceat Regina." And wished, that all they that heard her oration had drunk of the flood Lethe. And so her Majesty cheerfully departed to her lodging.[6]

Here the Queen addresses the army at Tilbury on the eve of the Armada. A ballad sets the scene.

Her Highness then to the camp did go,
The order there to see and know,
Which her Lord General did dutifully show
In Tilsbury camp in England:
And every captain to her came,
And every officer of fame,
To show their duty and their name
    To their sovereign Queen of England.
Of tents and cabins thousands three,
Some built with bows and many a tree,
And many of canvas she might see
    In Tilsbury camp in England.

* * *

To tell the joy of all and some

[6] From Francis Peck, *Desiderata Curiosa* (London, 1732), II, 25–44.

When that her Majesty was come,
Such playing on fifes and many a drum
 To welcome the Queen of England:
Displaying of ensigns very brave
Such throwing of hats, what would ye have?
Such cries of joy, God keep and save
 Our noble Queen of England!
And then to bid her Grace good night,
Great ordinance shot with pellet's pight,
Fourteen fair pieces of great might
 To tease the foes of England.[7]

The Queen's Speech[8]

My Loving People: We have been persuaded by some that are careful of our safety, to take heed how we commit ourselves to armed multitudes, for fear of treachery; but I assure you, I do not desire to live to distrust my faithful and loving people.

Let tyrants fear; I have always so behaved myself, that, under God, I have placed my chiefest strength and safeguard in the loyal hearts and good will of my subjects, and therefore, I am come amongst you, as you see, at this time, not for my recreation and disport, but being resolved in the midst and heat of the battle, to live or die amongst you all, to lay down for my God, and for my kingdoms, and for my people, my honor and my blood, even in the dust.

I know I have the body but of a weak and feeble woman; but I have the heart and stomach of a king, and of a king of England too; and think foul scorn that Parma or Spain, or any prince of Europe should dare to invade the borders of my realm; to which rather than any dishonor shall grow by me, I myself will take up arms, I myself will be your general, judge, and rewarder of every one of your virtues in the field.

I know already, for your forwardness you have deserved rewards and crowns; and we do assure you in the word of a prince, they shall be duly paid you. In the meantime, my lieutenant-general shall be

---

[7] From *Old Ballads from Early Printed Copies*, ed. J. P. Collier (London, 1840), pp. 110–17.

[8] From *Somers Tracts*, ed. W. Scott (London, 1809), I, 429–30.

in my stead, than whom never prince commanded a more noble or worthy subject; not doubting but by your obedience to my general, by your concord in the camp, and your valor in the field, we shall shortly have a famous victory over those enemies of my God, of my kingdoms, and of my people.

At the end of her reign, Sir John Harington remembered a conversation that aptly summarizes the Queen's long love affair with the people. The romance—or as Elizabeth preferred, the marriage—of Queen and people had survived 44 tumultuous years.

The Queen did once ask my wife in merry sort, how she kept my good will and love, which I did always maintain to be truly good towards her and my children? My Mall, in wise and discreet manner, told her Highness, she had confidence in her husband's understanding and courage, well founded on her own steadfastness not to offend or thwart, but to cherish and obey. Hereby did she persuade her husband of her own affection, and in so doing did command his.——"Go to, go to, mistress," saith the Queen, "you are wisely bent I find: after such sort do I keep the good will of all my husbands, my good people; for if they did not rest assured of some special love toward them, they would not readily yield me such good obedience." This deserveth noting, as being both wise and pleasant.[9]

[9] From *Nugae Antiquae*, ed. Thomas Park (London, 1804), pp. 177–78.

7

The Queen and Religion

The first and most difficult problem of the new reign was the religious question. The range of possibilities was wide and Elizabeth made the most of the uncertainty that surrounded her intentions. As the daughter of Anne Boleyn she appeared as a natural Protestant leader, and the Marian exiles came flocking home from Strassburg and Geneva to erect the new Jerusalem. But Elizabeth had practiced the mass under Mary and wanted to retain the Spanish alliance. She thus began to steer a middle course, not unlike that taken by her father. Was it out of religious conviction or political expediency? As always when we try to discover Elizabeth's motives, we must rest unsure; but there is no doubt that her ambiguous religious policies did serve to strengthen the crown and preserve her precarious position. If she has usually been thought a politique, *who is to say that in the recesses of her own conscience, religious conviction did not coincide with political purpose? In any case, like all parties of the sixteenth century, Elizabeth always represented God as behind her, even if in this case it was a relatively moderate and politic providence.*

The first measure of the Queen upon her accession was a proclamation forestalling preaching and reformation until Parliament could assemble. It was followed by two great statutes, the Acts of Supremacy and Uniformity, and a series of injunctions that established—or re-established—the Anglican Church. Most of the clergy acceded to the Act of Supremacy but virtually all the bishops resisted. They were deprived but some among them appealed directly to the Queen, who replied as follows.

Sirs, As to your entreaty, for us to listen to you, we wave it: yet do return you this our answer. Our realm and subjects have been long wanderers, walking astray, whilst they were under the tuition of Romish pastors, who advised them to own a wolf for their head (in lieu of a careful shepherd), whose inventions, heresies, and schisms be so numerous, that the flock of Christ have fed on poisonous shrubs for want of wholesome pastures. And whereas you hit us and our subjects in the teeth, that the Romish church first planted the catholic faith within our realms, the records and chronicles of our realms testify the contrary; and your own Romish idolatry maketh you liars: witness the ancient monument of Gildas; unto which both foreign and domestic have gone in pilgrimage there to offer. This author testifieth Joseph of Arimathea to be the first preacher of the word of God within our realms. Long after that, when Austin came from Rome, this our realm had bishops and priests therein, as is well known to the wise and learned of our realm by woeful experience, how your church entered therein by blood; they being martyrs for Christ, and put to death, because they denied Rome's usurped authority.

As for our father being withdrawn from the supremacy of Rome by schismatical and heretical counsels and advisers; who, we pray, advised him more, or flattered him, than you, good Mr. Heath, when you were bishop of Rochester? And than you, Mr. Bonner, when you were archdeacon? And you, Mr. Turberville? Nay further, who was more an adviser of our father, than your great Stephen Gardiner, when he lived? Are not you then those schismatics and heretics? If so, suspend your evil censures. Recollect, was it our sister's conscience made her so averse to our father's and brother's actions, as to undo what they had perfected? Or was it not you, or such like advisers, that dissuaded her, and stirred her up against us and other of the subjects?

And whereas you would frighten us, by telling how emperors, kings, and princes have owned the bishop of Rome's authority; it was contrary in the beginning. For our Saviour Christ paid his tribute unto Caesar, as the chief superior; which shows your Romish supremacy is usurped.

As touching the excommunication of St. Athanasius by Liberius and that council, and how the emperor consented thereunto; consider the heresies that at that time had crept into the church of Rome, and how courageously Athanasius withstood them, and how he got the victory. Do ye not acknowledge his creed to this day? Dare any of you say, he is a schismatic? Surely ye be not so audacious. Therefore as ye acknowledge his creed, it shows he was no schismatic. If Athanasius withstood Rome for her then heresies, then others may safely separate themselves from your church, and not be schismatics.

We give you warning, that for the future we hear no more of this kind, lest you provoke us to execute those penalties enacted for the punishing of our resisters: which out of our clemency we have forborne.[1]

But doctrine, even ceremony, continued to remain deliberately vague. Nor did the Queen dash the hopes of Philip II who thought to wed her, and the Pope who invited representation at the Council of Trent. She even kept a crucifix and lighted taper conspicuously in her private chapel. The letters of the returning Marian exiles to their continental friends describe the Queen's policy; they also show the writers' impatience and finally their distrust of Elizabeth. Here is the origin of a "puritan" party distinctly to the left of the Queen. As early as 1560, a letter reflects this uneasiness.

Thomas Sampson to Peter Martyr (1560)[2]

Oh! my father, what can I hope for, when the ministry of the word is banished from court? while the crucifix is allowed, with lights burning before it? The altars indeed are removed, and images also throughout the kingdom; the crucifix and candles are retained at court alone. And the wretched multitude are not only rejoicing at this, but will imitate it of their own accord. What can I hope, when three of our lately appointed bishops are to officiate at the table of the Lord, one as priest, another as deacon, and a third as subdeacon, before the image of the crucifix, or at least not far from it, with candles, and habited in the golden vestments of the

---

[1] From John Strype, *Annals of the Reformation* (Oxford, 1824), I, i, 218–19.
[2] From *The Zurich Letters*, 2nd series, ed. H. Robinson (London, 1845), I, 63–64.

papacy; and are thus to celebrate the Lord's supper without any sermon? What hope is there of any good, when our party are disposed to look for religion in these dumb remnants of idolatry, and not from the preaching of the lively word of God? What can I hope, when injunctions are laid upon those appointed to preach, not to handle vice with too much severity; when the preachers are deemed intolerable, if they say anything that is displeasing? But whither is my warmth of feeling carrying me away? I must be silent, though I have scarcely touched upon the heads of the misery that is hanging over us. Eternal Lord, have mercy on us, through Jesus Christ, our God and Saviour!

The Queen appointed Matthew Parker as her Archbishop of Canterbury. She gave him considerable latitude in purely religious matters but intervened from time to time when religious and political matters overlapped, as here in the question of discipline and uniformity.

The Queen to Parker (January 25, 1565)[3]

Most reverend Father in God, etc. We greet you well. Like as nothing, in the government and charge committed unto us by the favorable goodness of Almighty God, doth more profit and beautify the same to His pleasure and acceptation, to our comfort and ease of our government, and, finally to the universal weal and repose of our people and countries, than unity, quietness, and concord, as well amongst the public ministers having charge under us, as in the multitude of the people by us and them ruled; so, contrariwise, diversity, variety, contention, and vain love of singularity, either in our ministers or in the people, must needs provoke the displeasure of Almighty God, and be to us, having the burden of government, discomfortable, heavy, and troublesome; and, finally, must needs bring danger of ruin to our people and country. Wherefore, although our earnest care and inward desire hath always been, from

---

[3] From *The Correspondence of Matthew Parker*, ed. J. Bruce (London, 1853), pp. 223–27.

the beginning of our reign, to provide that by laws and ordinances agreeable to truth and justice, and consonant to good order, this our realm should be directed and governed, both in the ecclesiastical and civil policy, by public officers and ministers following, as near as possibly might be, one rule, form, and manner of order in all their actions, and directing our people to obey humbly and live godly, according to their several callings, in unity and concord, without diversities of opinions or novelties of rites and manners, or without maintenance or breeding of any contentions about the same; yet we, to our no small grief and discomfort do hear, that . . . in sundry places of our realm of late, for lack of regard given thereto in due time, by such superior and principal officers as you are, being the primate and other the bishops of your province, with sufferance of sundry varieties and novelties, not only in opinions but in external ceremonies and rites, there is crept and brought into the church by some few persons, abounding more in their own senses than wisdom would, and delighting with singularities and changes, an open and manifest disorder and offence to the godly wise and obedient persons by diversity of opinions. . . . And although we have now a good while heard to our grief sundry reports hereof, hoping that all cannot be true, but rather mistrusting that the adversaries of truth might of their evil disposition increase the reports of the same: yet we thought until this present, that by the regard which you, being the primate and metropolitan would have had hereto according to your office, with the assistance of the bishops your brethren in their several dioceses (having also received of us heretofore charge for the same purpose), these errors, tending to breed some schism or deformity in the church, should have been stayed and appeased. But perceiving very lately, and also certainly, that the same doth rather begin to increase than to stay or diminish, we, considering the authority given to us of Almighty God for defence of the public peace, concord, and truth of this his Church, and how we are answerable for the same to the seat of his high justice, mean not to endure or suffer any longer these evils thus to proceed, spread, and increase in our realm, but have certainly determined to have all such diversities, varieties, and novelties amongst them of the clergy and our people . . . to be reformed and repressed and brought to one manner of uniformity through our whole realm and dominions, that our people may thereby quietly honor and serve Almighty God in truth, concord, peace, and quietness, and thereby also avoid the slanders that are spread abroad hereupon in foreign countries.

And therefore, we do by these our present letters, require, enjoin and straitly charge you . . . to proceed by order, injunction, or censure, according to the order and appointment of such laws and ordinances as are provided by act of Parliament, and the true meaning thereof, so as uniformity of order may be kept in every church, and without variety and contention. . . . And if any superior officers shall be found hereto disagreeable, if otherwise your discretion or authority shall not serve to reform them, we will that you shall duly inform us thereof, to the end we may give indelayed order for the same; for we intend to have no dissension or variety grow by suffering of persons which maintain dissension to remain in authority; for so the sovereign authority which we have under Almighty God should be violate and made frustrate, and we might be well thought to bear the sword in vain.

Uniformity could only be achieved at the expense of a Catholic and Puritan opposition. The Queen's tactics delayed a crisis for a full decade while the Anglican Church struck new roots. But the more securely it was established, the more inevitable was the resistance. The most immediate danger was from the old religion. The focus of Catholic resistance was the North. As in Henry VIII's time, a combination of motives stirred rebellion there but it was Mary Stuart's captivity in England that sparked the rising of 1569. Mary was spirited off in the nick of time and the Queen's forces successfully defeated the rebels led by the Earls of Northumberland and Westmorland. In this crisis, the Queen felt the desirability of issuing a general defense of her rule. She issued a Declaration *after the rebellion justifying her policies of the past ten years.*

When we consider with ourselves, how it hath pleased Almighty God of his abundant goodness to bless his good creatures our subjects in all our dominions with such a general quietness and peace, as the like hath not been seen in these our kingdoms in many ages, until this last year (which was after the time of eleven years of our reign), that an unnatural commotion of certain of our subjects in a part of our realm in the North, was by certain lewd practices of some few secretly stirred up; and yet by God's goodness, with the faithfulness of our true subjects shortly suppressed and quieted: we find it necessary that, as we are most bound to render unto the same our good God the whole praise and honor for these his blessings upon us and our dominions, and for the same to continue thankful; so ought we also in respect of our princely charge, to consider both how this interruption of the course of so universal, long, and continual inward peace hath happened; and how also by God's favor and assistance it may be provided, that the like occasions hereafter be no ministered by seditious persons . . . .

*   *   *

We do [desire] all persons to understand, that of our own natural disposition (through God's goodness) we have been always desirous to have the obedience of all our subjects of all sorts, both high and low, by love and by compulsion; by their own yielding and not by our exacting; allowing that which was well said by a wise prince of the Greeks: "That king to be in most surety that so ruled over his subjects, as a father over the children." And therefore, by God's grace we may boldly say, that there is no one example in our whole dominions to be produced, that we ever by any means sought the life, the blood, the goods, the houses, states or lands of any person in any estate or degree; nor yet procured or suffered any division or discord to be stirred or maintained betwixt our nobility, amongst themselves, or betwixt one estate and other, for any our own avenge, profit, or pleasure. . . . [Nor are there] other causes that have been commonly afore times, and are to be seen in this time (the more to be lamented) offensive in some monarchies; as in wasting of all sorts of people by wilfull and continual wars, either foreign or civil; or impoverishing of the subjects by perpetual and new devised . . . exactions. We would it were well and justly considered, that first, we never yet began war with any prince or country, neither used force and arms but defensive; and not those at any time until such evident necessity (though not seen to the vulgar sort) compelled us either to prevent, or defend foreign forces, levied to the manifest danger of our realm; as, without such provisions, it was manifest that notable invasions had been made into the realm both by land and sea, and those so dangerous as no man's judgment can comprehend. In execution whereof, whatsoever extraordinary charges our good subjects either privately in service with their bodies, or commonly in contributions by subsidies, or such like (which as we know hath not been small, so yet neither so frequent nor grievous as hath been in sundry our progenitors' times, even to maintain wars abroad, fought, and long continued without necessity) manifest also it is, that we have of our own proper domain and revenues of our crown, not forborne to expend that which hath been both honorable and necessary. And the successes of these enterprises being well considered, none can justly say, that the realm hath lost any honor or interest thereby. We leave to all good and wise persons to consider by way of comparison, what difference is to be found, betwixt the security, the tranquility, the wealth, and all other worldly felicities, which our people do and may enjoy, and the contraries; as continual and universal bloodsheds, burnings, spoilings, murders, exactions and such like, properly conjoined with civil wars in other countries; all which we wish to cease, through the mercies of Almighty God.

It remaineth further to be considered . . . what we have done . . . in the profession of Christian Religion. . . . And in this part we would it were indifferently understood, that . . . we know no other authority, either given or used by us, as Queen and governor of this realm, than hath been by the law of God and this realm always due to our progenitors, sovereigns, and kings of the same; although true it is that this authority hath been in the time of certain of our progenitors, some hundred years past, as by laws, records and stories doth appear (and especially in the reign of our noble father, King Henry VIII, and our dear brother, King Edward VI) more clearly recognized by all the estates of the realm, as the like hath been in our time; without that thereby we do either challenge or take to us (as malicious persons do untruly surmise) any superiority to ourself to define, decide, or determine any article or point of the Christian faith and religion, or to change any ancient ceremony of the Church from the form before received and observed by the Catholic and

Apostolic Church, or the use of any function belonging to any ecclesiastical person being a minister of the word and sacraments in the Church: but that authority which is yielded to us and our crown consisteth in this: that, considering we are by God's grace and sovereignty, prince and queen, next under God, and all the people in our realm are immediately born subjects to us and our crown and to none else, and that our realm hath of long time past received the Christian faith, we are by this authority bound to direct all estates, being subject to us, to live in the faith and the obedience of Christian Religion, and to see the laws of God and man, which are ordained to that end, to be duly observed, and the offenders against the same duly punished, and consequently to provide, that the Church may be governed and taught by archbishops, bishops and ministers according to the ecclesiastical ancient policy of the realm, whom we do assist with our sovereign power, etc. . . . So as certainly no just occasion can hereby be taken to deprave our government in any causes ecclesiastical. And yet to answer further all malicious untruths dispersed abroad to induce a grudging of our government in this behalf, we know not, nor have any meaning to allow, that any our subjects should be molested either by examination, or inquisition, in any matter, either of faith, as long as they shall profess the Christian faith, not gainsaying the authority of the holy scriptures, and of the articles of our faith, contained in the creeds Apostolic, and Catholic; or for matter of ceremonies, or any other external matters appertaining to Christian Religion, as long as they shall in their outward conversation show themselves quiet and conformable, and not manifestly repugnant and obstinate to the laws of the realm, which are established for frequentation of divine service in the ordinary churches, in like manner as all other laws are, wherunto subjects are of duty and by allegiance bound.[4]

The rebellion of the earls was succeeded by a fresh and even more dangerous rebellion in the North, this time by Leonard Dacre. Although outnumbered, the Queen's forces

[4] From *A Collection of State Papers Left by William Cecil*, ed. Samuel Haynes (London, 1740), pp. 589–93.

triumphed. Here is the congratulatory postscript Elizabeth added to her letter to her kinsman Lord Hunsdon (February 26, 1570), expressing her relief at a close call.

I doubt much, my Harry, whether that the victory were given me more joyed me, or that you were by God appointed the instrument of my glory; and I assure you for my country's good, the first might suffice, but for my heart's contentation, the second more pleased me. It likes me not a little that, with a good testimony of your faith, there is seen a stout courage of your mind, that more trusted to the goodness of your quarrel than to the weakness of your number. . . . And that you may not think that you have done nothing for your profit, though you have done much for honor, I intend to make this journey somewhat to increase your livelihood, that you may not say to yourself, *perditur quod factum est ingrato.* Your loving kinswoman, E.R.[5]

Rather uncharacteristically, the Queen's anger was vented on many of the rebels who were hanged in large numbers, summarily as examples. It is one of the darker pages in her story.

We have always been more inclinable to mercy than to severity; so do we doubt whether at this time, an example being passed, as you know, in the necessary execution of justice upon a great number of the poorer sort of people, that have already worthily suffered death; it may not seem an inordinate compassion to have no greater example of justice upon the richer, than upon four only. We are pleased, that Henry Johnson, for his simplicity, and John Markenfeld, for his youth, and Ascolph Cleasby, at the request of you, our cousin of Hunsdon, shall be forborne from execution. And for the other four, Metcalf, Lambert, Claxton, and Conyers, we are in nothing moved to spare them, for any respect of the profit that might come to us by their life; and yet knowing

[5] From *Calendar of State Papers Domestic Elizabeth 1566–79 Addenda* (London, 1871), p. 246.

not of the manner and circumstance of their offence, how they have therein exceeded in any malice, we will not expressly command that they all shall suffer death; but, although we think it good that some further example be showed, we refer the same to your own judgment, either to cause all the rest of those four to suffer, or some of them, whom you shall understand to have most exceeded in malice and inordinate action, and thereby most unworthy of mercy; and to spare such other of them as you shall understand to have offended in the lesser degrees, until we may hereafter determine what shall be mete to be done with them.[6]

> *But severe as the Queen may have been, it was the civil disobedience and not the question of religious conviction that so offended her. As she argued in her* Declaration *above, she was deliberately tolerant as long as outward conformity and peace remained. Many Catholics thus found it possible to exist quietly in Elizabethan England. In 1570, Elizabeth declared through the Lord Keeper in Star Chamber, that she would never inspect consciences. But outward conformity was not easy to demand where the inward disposition was opposed, especially in an age of passionate religious conviction.*

Whereas certain rumors are carried and spread abroad among sundry her Majesty's subjects, that her Majesty hath caused, or will hereafter cause, inquisition and examination to be had of men's consciences in matters of religion; her Majesty would have it known, that such reports are utterly untrue, and grounded either of malice, or of some fear more than there is cause. For although certain persons have been lately convented before her Majesty's council upon just causes, and that some of them have been treated withal upon some matter of religion; yet the cause thereof hath grown merely of themselves; in that they have first manifestly broken the laws established for religion, in not coming at all to the church, to common prayer and divine service, as of late time before they were accustomed, and had used by the space of nine or ten whole years alto-

[6] Elizabeth to Lord Hunsdon, etc., March 31, 1570, in *Memorials of the Great Rebellion of 1569*, ed. Cuthbert Sharp (London, 1840), p. 228.

gether: so as if thereby they had not given manifest occasion by their open and wilful contempt of breaking of her Majesty's laws, they had not been anything molested, or dealt withal.

Wherefore, her Majesty would have all her loving subjects to understand, that, as long as they shall openly continue in the observation of her laws, and shall not wilfully and manifestly break them by their open actions, her Majesty's meaning is, not to have any of them molested by any inquisition or examination of their consciences in causes of religion; but will accept and entreat them as her good and obedient subjects. And if any shall otherwise by their open deeds and facts declare themselves wilfully disobedient to break her laws; then she cannot but use them according to their deserts; and will not forbear to inquire to their demeanors, and of what mind and disposition they are, as by her laws her Majesty shall find it necessary.[7]

The Counter-Reformation launched in Rome and supported by Philip II created new perils for Elizabeth. A papal bull excommunicated her in 1570; a Jesuit college was founded at Douai to train English priests to spread the faith at home. Most dangerous were the "Enterprise," which threatened foreign invasion, and the conspiracies that were directed at the Queen's life. In this context an increasing animosity to Catholics—or at least to Jesuits, whose activities appeared to be (and sometimes were) treasonable—was inevitable. New recusancy laws were passed, censorship tightened; Jesuits martyred. But even so, considerable numbers of Englishmen remained Catholic and peaceable. Here the Queen is seen encouraging an informer.

Lord Burghley to Several Members of the Council, August 30, 1592[8]

My very good lords, I have showed unto her Majesty your lordships' letters of the 28th of this month, and the declaration of

---

[7] From John Strype, *Annals of the Reformation* (Oxford, 1824), I, ii, 370–71.
[8] From John Strype, *Annals of the Reformation* (Oxford, 1824), IV, 147.

Yonge, now so named, the seminary priest. Which her Majesty, beside my report, was pleased to have both the letter and the declaration leisurely read to her by Robert Cecil: and none other present with her Majesty but myself. Upon your letter she hath conceived that your lordships have dealt very wisely and cunningly to procure him to open himself so liberally as he hath done.

Upon the declaration she findeth many matters worth to be marked. And she would Wiseman, Cole, and others named by him, to be apprehended; and charged with some other things, and not with relieving of this Yonge. Of whom she would have a general opinion conceived, that nothing can be had of himself: neither that it is like that he is acquainted with any matter of weight. So as he may retain his former credit with his complices; thereby to discover more recent matter. Her Majesty would not any here, of her council, know that part of his confession, but only myself and Robert Cecil, because seeing the length, to ease me, she caused him to read it.

If your lordships privately can induce him to remember more matter, especially to discover in what persons our rebels put their trust, assuring him of keeping the same secret, so as he should never be blamed for the same, her Majesty would greatly like it.

But the Catholics were only one half the problem; from 1570 or so the Puritans became increasingly hostile and provocative. About that time, there appeared two Admonitions to Parliament *attacking the whole religious establishment and calling for radical reform. The political hazards to Elizabeth's rule were now plain, and they account for her quick suppression of the two works. For the rest of the reign she had to cope with their criticism, and after 1583 she assisted her new Archbishop, John Whitgift, in ruthlessly suppressing them. But it was left to her successors to meet their full challenge. Undoubtedly Elizabeth was assisted here by the Catholic attack, which absorbed the energies of Protestants of all persuasions and left her the chief bulwark against the Counter-Reformation. Even so, the Puritans could be more than a minor nuisance, as their resistance to Elizabeth in*

Parliament (Chapter 11) illustrates. Here the Dean of York outlines the political problem that Elizabeth faced.

. . . At the beginning, it was but a cap and surplice, and a tippet; but now it is grown to Bishops, Archbishops, and Cathedral churches, and the overthrow of order established, and (to speak plain) to the Queen's Majesty's authority in causes ecclesiastical. The supreme authority (you know) in ecclesiastical causes was justly taken from the Pope, because he was an usurper, and given to the prince within his realm, to whom of right it doth appertain; but these reformers, take it from the prince, and give it unto themselves, with the grave seigniorie in every parish. For by them would they have every cause debated when any ariseth in the congregation. If they cannot end it, by the ministers and seigniorie of the parishes adjoining; if they cannot determine it, by a national council; if it cannot be ended there, then to be referred to a general council of all the churches reformed. They make no mention of the Queen's authority. I warrant you, she must draw forth her sword, and see that this order of theirs be observed and kept; and more she hath not to do, if we believe some of them. But to come nearer unto the matter, your Lordship doth understand right well, I doubt not, that of the late writers there are some, that think not very well of the supremacy of princes in all causes ecclesiastical, as Calvin, who, in the government of the church, ascribeth not so much to the civil magistrate. . . . We say, that the prince is . . . armed with the sword to defend both the Tables of Moses, and to see that both God be duly honored, and every man by his neighbor be well used; but also hath authority to abolish idolatry and superstition, to make and constitute ecclesiastical laws for the advancement of true worship of God; and if the ministers do not their duty to punish them and to displace them, and to appoint others more faithful and diligent in their rooms. We say also, that in civil and temporal things the prince is the vice regent of God, and representeth here in earth the person of God; and in scripture is called by the name of God, and that the majesty of a prince is a sacred thing, and therefore, that the prince's laws, both ecclesiastical and civil, not contrary to the word of God, but tending either to edify the Church, or to profit the commonweal, may not with the safe conscience be disobeyed of any subject. But some of these reformers speak more profanely of the prince, and say, that the prince ruleth in the commonwealth herself, and in the Church of God seeth that all be ruled of the Lord; whereas, indeed in both she ruleth but as vice regent, and seeth that both be ruled of the Lord; and it is an hard kind of doctrine to say, that the prince's laws, though they be good, yet bind not the conscience; seeing St. Paul exhorteth us to obey the superior power, not only for fear of punishment, but also for conscience sake.[9]

[9] Matthew Hutton to Burghley, October 6, 1573, in *A Collection of State Papers . . . at Hatfield House,* ed. William Murdin (London, 1759), pp. 261–66.

8

The Queen and Foreign Affairs

Next to religion, foreign policy presented the most pressing and continuous problem of the reign. Elizabeth was faced at once with the traditional hostility of France and Scotland combined. She clung therefore to the Spanish alliance while extricating herself from war with France. After some irresolution, she began also modestly to support the Protestant faction in Scotland. Although her policy appeared timid and uncertain to her advisers it brought peace, and thus time to strengthen the Queen's rule and pocketbook. Nevertheless relations with Spain began gradually to deteriorate. Religious antipathy was combined with national rivalry, particularly after the Papal excommunication of 1570. English ships, encouraged by the Crown, began to prey on Spanish commerce. Elizabeth supplied covert aid to the Netherlands in the revolt against Philip II. And Huguenots and Catholics were courted by both sides in a divided France. All the while Philip and the Pope began to plan the "Enterprise," an armed invasion of England. Still, war was averted for many years as a result of Elizabeth's many subterfuges and Philip's natural caution. The defeat of the Armada in 1588 released Elizabeth from immediate danger, although the Spanish threat remained. The Queen was now the acknowledged leader of Protestant Europe; her allies included James VI of Scotland and Henry of Navarre, who claimed the French Crown in 1589. Her strategy had been sanctioned by success. Only rebellion in Ireland remained a problem, draining Elizabeth's carefully protected coffers and threatening anew the solvency of the monarchy.

On the whole, Elizabeth's foreign policy was one of her greatest achievements. Her caution was matched by a subtlety and unscrupulousness that disarmed and confused her enemies. Her prudence kept her from the disasters that her bolder advisers would undoubtedly have created by their very rashness

*and bravado. The Queen made mistakes, of course, but her
female virtues were by and large more than a match for her
more blustering masculine contemporaries. The documents
that follow illustrate some of her diplomatic skills in dealing
with kings and ambassadors. Other aspects of her foreign
policy will be dealt with in subsequent chapters.*

*The Queen's dilemma in 1558 was succinctly put by a con-
temporary.*

The Queen poor; the realm exhausted; the nobility poor and
decayed; want of good captains and soldiers; the people out of
order; justice not executed; justices of peace unmeet for office; all
things dear; excess of meat and drink, and apparel; division among
ourselves; war with France and Scotland; the French King bestrid-
ing the realm, having one foot in Calais and the other in Scotland;
steadfast enmity, but no steadfast friendship abroad.[1]

*The dispatches of the Spanish ambassadors to Philip II
provide the most complete record of Elizabeth's diplomacy
in the first years of her reign. Here are some excerpts. In the
first, the Count de Feria reports a conversation of April 1559
in which the religious issue already appears a divisive force.*

I received your Majesty's letter of the 24th instant on the
27th and went to the palace the next day. After giving your Majesty's letter to the Queen, I spoke to her in conformity with what
had been written to me. She heard me as she had heard me many
times before, only that on this occasion I spoke in your Majesty's
name. Although I tried to frighten her all I could, I kept in view
the necessity of not offending her as they have preached to her
constantly that your Majesty and the King of France hold her of
small account, and she thinks that the only thing she needs is to
get rich. I smoothed her down a good deal in this respect making

[1] Armigil Waad, *Calendar of State Papers Foreign Elizabeth* (London, 1863),
IV, xviii, fn.

her understand that your Majesty was prompted only by your great affection for her and considered her harm or advantage as your own. She answered amiably that she thanked your Majesty for your message. Subsequently in conversation with me she said three or four very bad things. One was that she wished the [Lutheran] confession of Augsburg to be maintained in her realm, whereat I was much surprised and found fault with it all I could, adducing the arguments I thought might dissuade her from it. She then told me it would not be the Augsburg confession, but something else like it, and that she differed very little from us as she believed that God was in the sacrament of the Eucharist, and only dissented from three or four things in the Mass. After this she told me she did not wish to argue about religious matters. I told her neither did I. . . .

She then said that as these were matters of conscience, she should in life and death remain of the same way of thinking, and would be glad of three hours' talk with your Majesty. At the end of the colloquy she said she hoped to be saved as well as the Bishop of Rome. I told her of the good offices your Majesty had rendered to her with the Pope in order that he should not proceed against her, and asked her not to let them persuade her that this was a small matter, as for a schism less grave than heresy, a king of Navarre had been deprived of his kingdom by a sentence of the Pope, and remained without it to this day. I assured her that if the King of France had ordered her and the Council how to govern, they could not have acted more favorably for his ends than they had done, and as I saw the ruin of her and her realm and was grieved thereat, I could not refrain from telling her thus clearly and openly as she had heard me say many times before. . . . It is very troublesome to negotiate with this woman, as she is naturally changeable, and those who surround her are so blind and bestial that they do not at all understand the state of affairs.[2]

In 1564 a new Spanish Ambassador, Guzman de Silva, appeared at Elizabeth's court. He was royally entertained.

[2] From *Calendar of State Papers Spanish Elizabeth* (London, 1892), I, 61–63.

When I arrived at the house where the Queen was they showed me into a room until her Majesty knew of my arrival. She was walking in the garden with her ladies and sent the Lord Chamberlain for me to go to her. She raised me with a great show of pleasure, and said that her ardent wish to see me had caused her to give me this trouble, and that I was to forget that the Queen was there and look upon her as a private lady, the preparations not being hers but those of a friend and subject, although the house was well prepared and her nobles were round her. I answered that wherever monarchs were there was their regal state, as I perceived in this case. We then went up into a very large gallery, where she took me aside for nearly an hour, all her talk being about your Majesty, and on several occasions during the conversation she recalled events that had occurred when she had first come to the throne, telling them so minutely that I will not tire your Majesty by repeating them. She was so taken up with it that I think she was sorry when supper was announced. Speaking of France, she said that she had received a letter written in Lyons, from the Queen, brought by her Ambassador that morning, who had arrived at dinner time, and had had to wait. This was, I think, to satisfy me that she had not asked him to dinner. We then went to supper, which was served with great ceremony, as is usual here, and every attention and honor were shown to me. She ordered her musicians to play the *Battle of Pavia,* which she assured me was the music she enjoyed most. After supper she stayed talking to me for some time, and as it was already late I thought it was time to leave her. I was about to take my leave when she told me not to go yet, as she wished me to see a comedy that was to be acted. She said she would go into her chamber for a short time, and in the meanwhile Lord Robert was to entertain me.

*   *   *

The Queen came out to the hall, which was lit with many torches, where the comedy was represented. I should not have understood much of it if the Queen had not interpreted, as she told me she would do. They generally deal with marriage in the comedies, and she turned to me and asked again about your Majesty, and whether the Prince [Don Carlos] had grown. I told her he had, and after thinking awhile she said, "Well, everyone disdains me; I understand he is to be married to the Queen of Scots." I said, "Do not believe it your Majesty. His Highness has been so ill with constant fever and other maladies of late years that it has been impossible to think of his marriage, but now that he is well again people talk of these matters without knowledge. It is no new thing for great princes to be the subjects of gossip." "So true is that," said the Queen, "that they said in London the other day that the King, my brother, was sending an Ambassador to treat of the marriage of the Prince with me!"

The comedy ended, and then there was a masque of certain gentlemen who entered dressed in black and white, which the Queen told me were her colors, and after dancing awhile one of them approached and handed the Queen a sonnet in English, praising her. She told me what it said, and I expressed my pleasure at it. This ended the feast, and the Queen entered a gallery where there was a very long table with every sort and kind of preserves and candied fruits that can be imagined, according to the English custom. It must have been two in the morning, and the Queen had to return to Westminster by water, although it was very windy. She sent me back to my lodgings accompanied by the same gentleman as had brought me, as I had come by land.[3]

As relations with Spain cooled, Anglo-French negotiations were renewed with an eye toward an alliance against Philip II. In 1572, however, many of the Protestants of Paris were ruthlessly murdered in a plot involving the Crown. News of the Massacre of St. Bartholomew's Day reached Elizabeth, who reacted sternly. Nevertheless, political necessity overcame moral outrage and negotiations continued.

The King, for the greater pretended honor to the Queen, sendeth in December, Mauvissière, Ambassador to her, first, for con-

[3] From *Calendar of State Papers Spanish Elizabeth* (London, 1892), I, 367–68.

tinuance of amity; secondly, to be godmother to the infant, his daughter; and lastly, to pursue the request of marriage with the Duke d'Alençon. The answer she then made by her Ambassador there (to round him in the ear again by a second message, for his cruelty, and the many aggravations of it) was to this tenor: "That she was sorry to hear what she had heard of her good brother (the which sprung from her good-will to that amity). First, that great slaughter made in France, of noblemen and gentlemen, unconvicted, and untried, so suddenly, as it was said, at his command, seemed so much to touch the honor of her good brother, as she could not but with lamentation, and with tears of her heart, hear it of a prince so near allied unto her, and in a chain of indissoluble love knit unto her by league and oath. That being after exposed by a conspiracy and treason wrought against her good brother's person (which whether it were true or false, being in another prince's kingdom and jurisdiction, where she had nothing to do, she minded not to be curious), yet that they were not brought to answer to law and judgment, before they were executed, she heard it marvellously ill taken; as a thing of a terrible and dangerous example. And was sorry that her good brother was so ready to condescend to any such counsel, whose nature she took to be more humane and noble. But that when more was added unto it; that when women, children, maids, young infants, and sucking babes, were at the same time murdered, and cast into the river; and that liberty of execution was given to the vilest and basest sort of the populace, without punishment or revenge of such cruelty, done afterwards by law upon such cruel murderers of such: this increased her grief and sorrow in her good brother's behalf; that he should suffer himself to be led by such inhuman counsellors.

And now, since it did appear by all doings, both by the edicts and otherwise, that the rigor was used only against them of the religion reformed, whether they were of any conspiracy or no; and that, contrary to the edict of pacification so often repeated, they of the reformed religion were either driven to fly, or die, or to recant, or lose their offices; whereby it did appear by all accords now used by her good brother, that his scope and intent did tend only to subvert that religion that she did profess, and to root it out of the realm. At the least, all the strangers of all nations and religions did so interpret it. As might appear by the triumphs and rejoicings, set out, as well in the realm of France as in others. Which made, that it must needs seem strange, both to her and to all others, that her good brother should require her to be godmother to his dear child, she being of that religion which he did now persecute, and could not abide within his realm. And that if she should believe the persuasion of others, and the opinion of all strangers her friends, who were not her subjects, she should in no case condescend to any association in that or any other matter.

But as she had always hitherto, as she concluded, had a special love to her good brother in his younger age, and a desire to the continuation of his good estate and quietness, which she had indeed manifestly showed, never seeking any advantage of trouble against him. . . . That notwithstanding that doubt and impediment before mentioned, she intended to send a worthy personage, a nobleman of her realm, to repair to his court, to visit the King, her good brother, and the Queen-mother; and to do that office which was required. Wishing that these spiritual alliances might be to their comfort, and to the conservation of the amity begun between them.[4]

Elizabeth's frugality was the despair of her advisers, especially in foreign affairs. But while it inhibited certain kinds of action, it kept the monarchy solvent—an overriding consideration for the Queen. Here an adviser criticizes her for it with unusual frankness. Francis Walsingham saw an opportunity for Elizabeth to invest in the fortunes of a candidate for the vacant Portugese monarchy named Don Antonio. Since Philip II also desired the crown (and secured it in 1581), Portugal represented another source of contention for the two powers. As Philip supported rebellion against Elizabeth in Ireland, so now Elizabeth was able to use Portugal against Philip. "We think it good for the King of Spain to be impeached both in Portugal and also in the Low Countries," Elizabeth wrote (July 22, 1581), "whereto we shall be ready to give such indirect assistance as shall not be a cause of war." A war "underhand" was all right, but it must be a war limited and unannounced.

[4] From John Strype, *Annals of the Reformation* (Oxford, 1824), II, i, 248–49.

Francis Walsingham to the Queen[5]

Sometimes when your Majesty doth behold in what doubtful terms you stand with foreign princes, then do you wish, with great affection, that opportunities offered had not been slipped. But when they are offered to you (if they be accompanied with charges), they are altogether neglected. Common experience teacheth, that it is as hard in a politic body to prevent any mischief without charges, as in a natural body, diseased, to cure the same without pain. Remember, I humbly beseech your Majesty, the respect of charges hath lost Scotland, and I would to God I had no cause to think that it might put your Highness in peril of the loss of England. I see it, and they stick not to say it, that the only cause that maketh them here not to weigh your Majesty's friendship, is, that they see your Majesty doth fly charges, otherwise than by doing them underhand. It is strange, considering in what state your Majesty standeth, that in all directions that we have here received, we have special charge not to yield to anything that may be accompanied with charges.

The general league must be without any certain charges; the particular league, with a voluntary and no certain charge; as also that which is to be attempted in favor of Don Antonio. The best is, that if they were (as they are not) inclined to deal in any of these points, then they were like to receive but small comfort for anything that we have direction to assent unto. Heretofore your Majesty's predecessors, in matters of peril, did never look into charges, though their treasure was neither so great as your Majesty's is, nor their subjects so wealthy, nor so willing to contribute. A person that is diseased, if he look only upon the medicine, without regard of the pain he sustaineth, cannot in reason and nature but abhor the same; if, therefore, no peril, why then 'tis vain to be at charges, but if there be peril, it is hard that charges should be preferred before peril. . . .

And, therefore, nothing being done to help the same, it is a

[5] From *The Compleat Ambassador*, ed. Dudley Digges (London, 1655), pp. 426–27.

manifest argument that the peril that is like to grow thereby is so fatal, as it can by no means be prevented, if this sparing and improvident course be still held, the mischiefs approaching being so apparent as they are. I conclude, therefore, having spoken in the heat of duty, without offence to your Majesty, that no one that serveth in the place of a counsellor, that either weigheth his own credit, or carrieth that sound affection to your Majesty as he ought to do, that would not wish himself in the furthest part of Ethiopia, rather than enjoy the fairest palace in England. The Lord, therefore, direct your Majesty's heart to take that way of counsel that may be most for your safety and honor.

The failure of the Spanish Armada created a new diplomatic atmosphere. A triumphant Queen could now address her younger contemporaries from the twin vantage points of success and age. She continued to influence Scottish affairs and to irritate James VI with a constant stream of advice and criticism. The King's restraint in replying stemmed largely from his natural caution, as well as his desire to succeed Elizabeth to the English throne (and therefore not to offend her).

Bishop Goodman recalls their relationship.

The Queen, having ever had a great and a high hand in governing of and managing the affairs in Scotland (insomuch that the Queen of Scots was wont to say, that Queen Elizabeth governed as much in Scotland as she did in England), did sometimes take occasion to require some things of the King of Scots only to accustom him to his obedience, whereupon the Lord-Treasurer Burghley sends for Mr. James Hudson, to the court. . . . And coming thither the Queen called for a box whereof she herself had the key, and whilst she was opening the box, she told Mr. Hudson, there was never a man in England did know the secrets she had in that box. Then taking pen and paper, she told Mr. Hudson she would have him to go into Scotland upon this business; that whereas she heard that Lennox was lately come over, and that he was born in France and held correspondence with the French, she thought it not fit that Edinburgh Castle should be committed to his custody, and therefore wished the King to remove him and appoint some other; that she would not write unto him to that purpose, but only left it to him to do the message; yet she wrote a letter to this effect. "This bearer is our subject born, and your servant sworn, repose trust in him for any message he shall deliver unto you." Mr. Hudson went instantly into Scotland, and knowing it to be an ungrateful message unto his master, and being sorry that he should be the messenger, he thought fit to lodge in the suburbs, and not to see the King for the four first days, yet it being known that he was in town, they might conceive that he was there upon occasion of some private business of his own. So after four days he came into the court, pretending no business at all; at length speaking with the King in private, he delivered his letter, desiring his Majesty to pardon him, that he was the messenger, and then delivered his message fully.

The King fell into a great chafe, as indeed for the instant he was very apt for passion, but after a little deliberation he was as temperate as any man living. At first he brake out into these words: "What hath the Queen to do with me? Why should not I dispose of my own as fully as she doth of hers? Why should I disgrace my near kinsman or why shall I show myself an inconstant wavering man? It may fall out in time that I shall give nothing without the Queen's leave." But after this passion was over, Mr. Hudson put him in mind how often he had promised and engaged himself to observe the Queen more than all the princes living; that old ladies must not be displeased for small matters; that his Majesty might gratify his kinsman some other way: then he told his Majesty that the occasion of his staying in town so long from his Majesty was, that no notice may be taken of his message. . . .[6]

> *Elizabeth's relations with Henry of Navarre also had their ups and downs. Here she upbraids him for accepting Catholicism as the price for confirming his title of King of France (1593). Her own conversion under Mary Tudor was quite forgotten.*

[6] From *The Court of King James I,* ed. J. S. Brewer (London, 1839), pp. 12–14.

Alas! what deep sorrow, what vehement grief, what sighs have I felt at my heart for the things which Morlante hath told me of? Alas! is the world come to this pass? Was it possible that any worldly matter should make you quit the fear of God? Can we expect any happy issue of such a fact? Or could you think that he who hath hitherto with his own right hand upholden and preserved you, would now forsake you? It is a very dangerous thing to do evil that good may come of it. Yet I hope a sober spirit will put you into a better mind. In the meantime I will not omit to make it a principal part of my prayers, the recommending you to God, beseeching him that the hands of Esau may not lose you the blessing of Jacob. Whereas you do religiously and solemnly offer me your friendship; I know to my great cost I have well deserved it: neither should I repent that, had you not changed your Father. Verily from henceforth I cannot be your sister by the Father; for the truth is, I shall ever more dearly love and honor mine own Father, than a false and counterfeit one: which God knoweth very well, who (I beseech him) bring you back again to a better mind. [Subscribed.] Your sister, if it be after the old manner; as for the new, I have nothing to do with it. Elizabeth R.[7]

In her old age the Queen remained in every respect an accomplished diplomat. Here her skills are applauded in different ways by two of the cleverest politicians in Europe, her Secretary of State, Robert Cecil, and the Duc de Sully, Henry IV's principal minister. In the first we see her wit (and Latin), in the second her over-all grasp of policy.

Robert Cecil to the Earl of Essex (1597)[8]

There arrived three days since in the city an ambassador out of Poland, a gentleman of excellent fashion, wit, discourse, language, and person; the Queen was possessed by some of our new

[7] From William Camden, *The History of Elizabeth*, 3rd ed. (London, 1675), p. 475.

[8] From *Queen Elizabeth and Her Times*, ed. Thomas Wright (London, 1838), pp. 478–80.

counsellors, that are as cunning in intelligence as in deciphering, that his negotiation tendeth to a proposition of peace. Her Majesty, in respect that his father the Duke of Finland had so much honored her, besides the liking she had of this gentleman's comeliness and qualities, brought to her by report, did resolve to receive him publicly, in the chamber of presence, where most of the earls and noblemen about the Court attended, and made it a great day. He was brought in attired in a long robe of black velvet, well jewelled and buttoned, and came to kiss her Majesty's hands where she stood under the state, from whence he straight returned ten yards off, and then began his oration aloud in Latin, with such a gallant countenance, as in my life I never beheld. The effect of it was this, that the King hath sent him to put her Majesty in mind of the ancient confederacies between the Kings of Poland and England; that never a monarch in Europe did willingly neglect their friendship, that he had ever friendly received her merchants and subjects of all quality, that she had suffered his to be spoiled without restitution, not for lack of knowledge of the violences, but out of mere injustice, not caring to minister remedy, notwithstanding many particular petitions and letters received, and to confirm her disposition to avow these courses (violating both the law of nature and nations) because there were quarrels between her and the King of Spain, she therefore took upon her, by mandate, to prohibit him and his countries, assuming thereby to herself a superiority (not tolerable) over other princes, nor he determined to endure, but rather wished her to know, that if there were no more than the ancient amity between Spain and him, it were no reason to look that his subjects should be impeded, much less now, when a strict obligation of blood had so conjoined him with the illustrious house of Austria; concluding that if her Majesty would not reform it, he would.

To this I swear by the living God, her Majesty made one of the best answers extempore, in Latin, that ever I heard, being much moved to be so challenged in public, especially against her expectation. The words of her beginning were these: ". . . Is this the business your King has sent you about? Surely I can hardly believe, that if the King himself were present, he would have used such language, for if he should, I must have thought that his being a King of not many years, and that not of blood but elected, indeed, newly elected, may leave him uninformed of that course which his father and ancestors have taken with us, and which, peradventure, shall be observed by those that shall come to live after him. And as for you," saieth she to the Ambassador, "although I perceive you have read many books, to fortify your arguments in this case yet I am apt to believe that you have not lighted upon the chapter that prescribeth the form to be used between kings and princes; but were it not for the place you hold, to have so publicly an imputation thrown upon our justice, which as yet never failed, we would answer this audacity of yours in another style; and for the particulars of your negotiations, we will appoint some of our Council to confer with you, to see upon what ground this clamor of yours hath his foundation, who showed yourself rather an herald than an ambassador."

I assure your Lordship, though I am not apt to wonder, I must confess before the living Lord that I never heard her (when I knew her spirits were in a passion) speak with better moderation in my life.

The Duc de Sully[9]

[1601] The Queen of England hearing the King was at Calais, thought it a favorable opportunity to satisfy her impatience of seeing and embracing her best friend. Henry was not less desirous of this interview, that he might confer with the Queen upon the affairs of Europe in general, as well as on their own in particular, especially those which had been just hinted to him by the English and Dutch ambassadors when he was at Nantes. Elizabeth first wrote him a letter equally polite and full of offers of service; she afterwards made him the usual compliments, and repeated those assurances by the Lord Edmund, whom she dispatched to Calais, till she herself could arrive at Dover, from whence she sent the Lord Sidney with other letters.

Henry resolving not to be outdone in complaisance, answered these advances in a manner that showed at once his respect for the sex of Elizabeth, and his esteem and admiration of her character. This intercourse continued a long time, to the great mortification

[9] From Duc de Sully, *Memoirs*, trans. Charlotte Lennox (London, 1756), II, 68–73.

of the Spaniards, whose jealousy was strongly excited by proximity and close correspondence. Of all the letters wrote by these two sovereigns on this occasion, I am possessed only of that in which Elizabeth informs the King of those obstacles that prevented her conferring with him in person, lamenting the unhappiness of princes, who, contrary to their inclinations, were slaves to forms and fettered by circumspection. This letter, because it was the occasion of the voyage I made to this princess, I have kept in my hands; in it she tells her most dear and well beloved brother (for so she called the King of France) that her concern at not being able to see him was so much the greater, as she had something to communicate to him which she durst not confide to any other person or commit to paper, and yet that she was upon the point of returning to London.

The King's curiosity was strongly excited by these last words; in vain did he torture his imagination to guess their purport. Secretary Feret being sent by him to fetch me, "I have just now received letters," said he to me, "from my good sister the Queen of England, whom you admire so greatly; they are more full of flatteries than ever: see if you will have more success than I have had in discovering her meaning." I agreed with Henry that it must be something of great consequence which induced her to express herself in this manner; it was resolved, therefore, that I should embark the next day for Dover, as if with no other design than to take advantage of the shortness of the passage to make a tour to London, which would give me an opportunity of seeing what step the Queen would take upon my arrival, neither the King nor I doubting but that she would be immediately informed of it. I acquainted no one with my intended passage, but such of my domestics as were to attend me, and of these I took but a very small number.

*   *   *

"It is well, M. de Rosny," said this Princess to me as soon as I appeared, "it is thus that you break our fences and pass on without coming to see me; I am greatly surprised at it, for I thought you bore me more affection than any of my servants, and I am persuaded that I have given you no cause to change those sentiments." I replied in few words, but such as so gracious a reception required. After which I began, without any disguise, to entertain her with those sentiments the King my master had for her. "To give you a proof," replied she, "that I believe all you have told me of the goodwill of the King my brother, and of your own, I will discourse with you on the subject of the last letter I wrote to him; though perhaps you have seen it, for Stafford (that is the name of the Lord Sidney) and Edmund tell me, that the King conceals few of his secrets from you." She then drew me aside, that she might speak to me with the greatest freedom, on the present state of affairs in Europe; and this she did with such strength and clearness, beginning from the Treaty of Vervins, that I was convinced this great Queen was truly worthy of that high reputation she had acquired in Europe. She entered into this detail, only to show me how necessary it was that the King of France should, in concert with her, begin to execute those great designs which they both meditated against the House of Austria. The necessity of this she founded upon the accessions this House was daily seen to make: she repeated to me all that had passed on this subject in 1598, between the King and the English and Dutch ambassadors, and asked me if this prince did not still continue to have the same sentiments, and why he so long delayed to begin the enterprise.

* * *

It was easy for the Queen of England to comprehend, by the manner in which I expressed myself, that these were not so much my own as Henry's sentiments which I communicated to her, and she gave me to understand as much, by confessing, that they appeared so just and reasonable to her, that she could not avoid adopting them: adding only, that there was one point on which all the parties could not be too soon agreed, which was, that the ultimate view of the intended combination being to confine the power of the House of Austria within just bounds, it would be necessary that each of the allies should so proportion all his desires or expectations which he might conceive in consequence of the event, as that none of them might be capable of giving umbrage to the rest: supposing, for example, that Spain should be deprived of the Low Countries, neither the whole nor any part of this State was to be coveted, either by the King of France, or the King of Scotland, who would one day become so of Great Britain, nor yet by the Kings of Sweden and Denmark, already sufficiently powerful by sea and land to make themselves respected by the other allies; and that the same conduct ought to be observed with regard to all the other spoils that might be taken from the House of Austria by those princes whose dominions should happen to be nearest to the conquered countries; "For if my brother, the King of France," said she, "should think of making himself proprietor, or even only feudal lord of the United Provinces, I should never consent to it, but entertain a most violent jealousy of him; nor should I blame him, if, giving him the same occasion, he should have the same fears of me."

These were not the only reflections made by the Queen of England; she said many other things, which appeared to me so just and sensible, that I was filled with astonishment and admiration. It is not unusual to behold princes form great designs; their sphere of action so forcibly inclines them to this, that it is only necessary to warn them of the extreme, which is, the projecting what their powers are so little proportioned to perform, that they scarce ever find themselves able to execute the half of what they proposed; but to be able to distinguish and form only such as are reasonable; wisely to regulate the conduct of them; to foresee and guard against all obstacles in such a manner, that when they happen, nothing more will be necessary, than to apply the remedies prepared long before. This is what few princes are capable of. Ignorance, prosperity, luxury, vanity, nay, even fear and indolence, daily produce schemes, to execute which there is not the least possibility. Another cause of surprise to me, was, that Elizabeth and Henry, having never conferred together on their political project, should agree so exactly in all their ideas, as not to differ even in the most minute particulars.

The Queen observing my eyes were attentively fixed on her without speaking, imagined she had expressed herself so confusedly in something she had said; that I was unable to comprehend her meaning. But when I ingenuously confessed to her the true cause of my silence and surprise, she then, without scruple, entered into the most minute parts of the design: but as I shall have an ample occasion to treat of this, in relating the great schemes which were prevented by the untimely death of Henry IV, I shall not trouble the reader with useless repetitions; but in this place just show the five principal points to which her Majesty reduced so extensive a scheme, as from the sequel of these Memoirs this will appear to have been. The first was, to restore Germany to its ancient liberty, in respect to the election of its emperors, and the nomination of a King of the Romans. The second, to render the United Provinces absolutely independent of Spain; and to form them into a republic, by annexing to them, if necessary, some provinces dismembered from Germany. The third, to do the same in regard to Switzerland, by incorporating with it some of the adjacent provinces, particularly Alsace and Franche-Comté. The fourth, to divide all Christendom into a certain number of powers, as equal as may be. The fifth, to reduce all the various religions in it under those three which should appear to be most numerous and considerable in Europe.

Our conference was very long: I cannot bestow praises upon the Queen of England that would be equal to the merit which I discovered in her in this short time, both as to the qualities of the heart and the understanding. . . .

9

The Queen and the Succession

The marriage of princes, in the sixteenth century, always had political consequences; it was therefore, to some extent, everybody's business. Yet marriage was also personal and individual. For Elizabeth a wedding promised two possible political consequences: it could produce an heir and insure a peaceful succession; it could be used to further her foreign policy by securing an alliance. Elizabeth had had suitors as a princess. Once, perhaps, she had been in love. Now as Queen she was more desirable than ever and suitors were attracted from all over Europe. They included Philip II, the Austrian princes Ferdinand and Charles, Prince Eric of Sweden, the Scottish Earl of Arran, and two brothers of the French King, the Dukes of Anjou and Alençon. At home, the most prominent was the Earl of Leicester. Nor does this exhaust the list.

But she refused them all, one by one. Often the courtship was protracted; at times all England debated the prospects. The pressure upon her was intense; she received advice— unsolicited as a rule—from her council, her church, her parliaments, and her subjects. Most argued for marriage and an heir. The prospects of the reign and the reformation seemed too tenuous to risk on a single person's life. But Elizabeth resisted; she died still the Virgin Queen.

Why? As always with Elizabeth, we can only conjecture. Was the reason as some have suggested, psychological? Did Elizabeth have an aversion to men, a result, among other things, of her mother's execution at the hands of Henry VIII? Or was it political? Did Elizabeth sacrifice the desires of her heart for the demands of the crown? Certainly in each particular case, there were always hard practical arguments to be made against the match. And, if sometimes she acted genuinely like a woman in love—with Leicester, for example, or the Duc d'Alençon—Elizabeth was always a consummate actress. Of two things only we can be sure: Elizabeth enjoyed being courted, and she milked every courtship for its political profit. Whatever her emotional life, she kept it hidden and restrained. In the long run, even the lack of an heir redounded to her advantage, for the Queen's life came every year to seem more precious to her subjects and their support therefore more assured.

Immediately upon her accession, Elizabeth was urged to marry. Here Archbishop Parker offers what was undoubtedly the prevailing view.

Furthermore, most sovereign Lady, as in most loyal obedience and duty of allegiance to your Highness, we thought it part of our pastoral office, to be solicitous in that cause which all your loving subjects so daily sigh for and morningly in their prayers desire to appear to their eyes. Marriage we all wish to see your godly affection inclined to, whereby your noble blood might be continued to reign over us to our great joy and comfort, whereby the great fears of ruin of this your ancient empire might be prevented, the destruction of your natural-born subjects avoided. We cannot but fear this continued sterility in your Highness' person to be a great token of God's displeasure toward us. The greatest part of your most assured faithful subjects secretly rejoiceth with thanks to God, to see your reign hitherto so prosperous, the rather for the establishing of God's pure religion again amongst us, but all your natural subjects in general most effectuously do crave at your hand to see you entered into the blessed state of wedlock, whereby your Highness' establishment and their assurance might be fully concluded: the hollow-hearted subject feedeth his hope only in this delay.[1]

At about the same time, Thomas Smith wrote a dialogue discussing her alternatives. It begins thus:

After dinner they were disposed to walk into my rude garden, and there, I cannot tell well who, one began to tell, that now of

[1] From *The Correspondence of Matthew Parker*, ed. J. Bruce (London, 1853), p. 131.

fresh the rumor of the King of Sweden Ericus' coming hither, (for as you know by the death of his father Gustave, it began to be stayed), was renewed again, and that of many he was undoubtedly looked for shortly to come himself hither into England, and in proper person, not by embassage, to be a wooer to her Majesty. Then, quoth I, would that wooing were once done, and that her Majesty had one whom she could like of, that we might see the hope and fruit of succession more near at hand. What said one of them, is there not in England as goodly men, noble, witty, and courageous, as be in other strange places? What need it be sought so far, that we have so near? By my troth, quoth another of them, methinketh far more better and honorable for all purposes, that her Majesty should take to husband some prince or nobleman, a stranger, than any of her own subjects. Well, saith the third, and I am in that mind (although I know it is not the most plausible opinion), that her Majesty doth best to keep her thus sole, unmarried as she is. The fourth at that was as much displeased as you were. Neither, saith he, am I altogether proselyte of the first opinion, nor yet of the second; but so that her Majesty marry, whether our countryman or a stranger, I like indifferently: marry, to hold that she should not marry, I hold it an unnatural, and in manner a wicked opinion against our country. My masters, quoth I, we have all leisure, thanks be to God, and you may make me now glad: for methinks I am in Plato's Academy, or Cicero's Tusculane. I pray you, seeing you all four be of divers opinions, let us hear your reasons. We can have no better place nor time; and if this green bank be not soft enough, we will have cushions brought to sit on. . . .[2]

The ˜Spanish ambassador, Feria, was commissioned to broach the possibility of a match with Philip II. He brought the subject up discreetly, but when the Queen launched a characteristic speech on her maidenhood he saw that she wished to "shelve the business," and changed the subject. The Archduke Ferdinand was then suggested—the son of the Emperor and a relative of Philip's—but the Queen temporized.

[2] From John Strype, *Life of Sir Thomas Smith* (Oxford, 1820), p. 63.

*"Sometimes she appears to want to marry him," Feria wrote;
but there were those who thought she loved Robert Dudley.
To complicate matters, his spies reported that "for a certain
reason which they have recently given me," Elizabeth would
not bear children. Still, he concluded optimistically, "if the
Archduke is a man, even if she should die without any, he will
be able to keep the kingdom with the support of your Majesty." Negotiations began but proceeded fruitlessly. Feria
reports.*

. . . At first she began, as usual, with words full of hope, but
seeing that these did not satisfy me, she drew back saying that she
did not think of marrying, although she might alter her mind when
she had seen the Archduke. I said that this intention did not
justify her in giving leave for the Archduke to come and see her,
and she answered that what she intended was only to see and know
him now, for when she might feel inclined to marry. I told her
that that was the time to see him, as I did not expect she would
marry in such haste when she did make up her mind as to lack
time to inform the princes who had to be consulted. She answered
that she wanted to act paradoxically in the matter, and to get
married before anyone in the world knew of it; whereupon I said,
seeing it was useless to dispute anymore, that if she thought of
doing it in that way there was no need that your Majesty's servants
should trouble her anymore about it. She did not like me to be un-
deceived already, as she well knows the danger which may arise,
and told me that she would think over what had better be done. I
asked her that communications on the matter should be made to
the Emperor's ambassador in my presence. The next day they
summoned us, and when we three were together I saw she still
wished to justify herself, so I determined to tell her what I had
hitherto withheld, namely, what Lady Sidney and her brother
and Treasurer Parry had told us, without mentioning their names.
I said that although no one would believe that so wise and prudent
a Princess would bring the Archduke over only to reject him,
yet we should not have dared to write to the Emperor as we had if
some of the principal persons of her court had not assured us that
she would marry him when he came, and these persons had in-

formed us that they took this step by her orders, as she had refrained from telling us herself from modesty; and we therefore wished for a more definite declaration from her than hitherto, now that in all probability the Archduke was on his way. I thought this would have excited her greatly, as was to be expected if it were not true, or at least if it were true that she would have put on some appearance of indignation. But this was not the case, for without even asking who the persons referred to were, she answered that someone had done this with good intentions, but without any commission from her. We were rather aggrieved at this, as we saw the trick had not been played by her alone. . . .[3]

It was soon clear to the Venetian Ambassador, at least, that the Queen was simply using her suitors for her own ends.

The Queen is by nature high spirited and has become yet more so owing to her good fortune and to the many physical and moral endowments which she possesses; so she has lofty designs, and promises herself success in all of them. She has many suitors for her hand, and by protracting any decision keeps them all in hope, persuading herself that in her need they will do what they can from rivalry to gain her love and matrimonial alliance.[4]

The succession problem was dramatically illustrated when in 1562, the Queen became dangerously ill. Ambassador Quadra advised King Philip.

The Queen was at Hampton Court on the 10th instant, and feeling unwell thought she would like a bath. The illness turned out to be small-pox, and the cold caught by leaving her bath for the air resulted in so violent a fever that on the seventh day she was

[3] From *Calender of State Papers Spanish Elizabeth* (London, 1892), I, 112–13.
[4] From *Calendar of State Papers Spanish XIII*, ed. Royal Tyler (London: Her Majesty's Stationers Office, 1954), pp. 220–21. Reprinted by permission of the Controller of Her Britannic Majesty's Stationery Office.

given up, but during that night the eruption came out and she is now better.

There was great excitement that day in the palace, and if her improvement had not come soon some hidden thoughts would have become manifest. The Council discussed the succession twice, and I am told there were three different opinions. Some wished King Henry's will to be followed and Lady Catherine declared heiress. Others who found flaws in the will were in favor of the Earl of Huntingdon. Lord Robert, the Earl of Bedford, the Earl of Pembroke, and the Duke of Norfolk with others of the lower rank were in favor of this. The most moderate and sensible tried to dissuade the others from being in such a furious hurry, and said they would divide and ruin the country unless they summoned jurists of the greatest standing in the country to examine the rights of the claimants, and in accordance with this decision the Council should then unanimously take such steps as might be best in the interests of justice and the good of the country. The Marquis Treasurer (Winchester) was of this opinion with others, although only a few, as the rest understood that this was a move in favor of the Catholic religion, nearly all the jurists who would be called upon to decide being of that faith, and this delay would give time for your Majesty to take steps in the matter which is the thing these heretics fear most, for upon your Majesty's absence they found all their hopes.

During this discussion the Queen improved. . . .[5]

Some years later negotiations for the Austrian match were brought to a conclusion. In any case, new stars had begun to appear in the firmament, the sons of Catherine de Medici, brothers of the King of France. By 1570 the time was propitious; Elizabeth had begun to fall out with Spain and look hopefully to France. However, with the older son, the Duc d'Anjou, negotiations stuck on the problem of religion. Not long afterward (1574) he succeeded to the French throne as Henry III. Elizabeth wrote to Walsingham, May 11, 1571.

[5] October 25, 1562. From *Calendar of State Papers Spanish Elizabeth* (London, 1892), I, 262–63.

. . . We find more great and urgent causes to move us to
persist in our former answer in the Article of Religion, both for
our conscience, our safetly, honor, and quietness, than can be alleged
or imagined for the conscience and honor of Monsieur de Anjou,
and the reasons hereof as apparent in this sort following: first, if
we shall grant a permission to Monsieur to have the use of his
religion, which we take principally to consist in the having, saying,
and hearing of the private mass, though the same should be secret
for the place, and rarely for the time, and not frequented with
numbers; yet it might seem doubtful to us how without offence of
conscience, such a toleration might be by us permitted. Secondarily,
though our conscience should not be offended, yet we are well
assured that our realm being not void of diversities of opinions
herein, though indeed presently we find no disobedience worthy of
any account against our laws, there could not any such exercise of
religion be used by our sufferance (by a person of such estimation,
as one being allowed to be our husband, should be) but that the
same would breed such a misliking to our best subjects and servants, as surely should diminish their great love toward us, and
consequently hazard some inward troubles within our realm. . . .[6]

> *For the younger son, the Duc d'Alençon, religion was less
> important, but extreme youth and an unattractive person
> created difficulties. Here, the Queen describes her reaction to
> the French ambassadors.*

And so our answer to them at their departure was this: that we
found such difficulties in this matter, especially for the difference of
his age, as presently we could not digest the same; but such was the
importunacy of our own subjects of all estates to have us to marry,
as we would forbear to give any such resolute answer as might
miscontent the said ambassador, and as we knew would much grieve
our people at this time, and so we would take some further time
to be advertised of the matter. And after one month's space we

[6] From *The Compleat Ambassador*, ed. Dudley Digges (London, 1655), pp.
97–98.

would make a direct answer to the French King, which also we would first communicate to the said Duke of Montmorency, to be by him, if he so would, delivered over to the said King. And so with this answer they departed; whereupon after the return of our Admiral, we have considered with him, and with some others that were there, by whom we find that indeed the conditions and the qualities of the said Duke as far forth as they could by their observation gather, or by report of others understand, were nothing inferior to M. de Anjou, but rather better to be liked; but as to his visage and favor, everybody doth declare the same to be far inferior, and that especially for the blemishes that the small pox hath wrought therein, so as his young years considered, the doubtfulness of the liking of his favor joined therewith, wherein nobody that hath seen him can otherwise report, although otherwise to all purposes he is commended before his brother; we cannot indeed bring our mind to like of this offer, especially finding no other great commodity offered to us with him, whereby the absurdity that in the general opinion of the world might grow, to commend this our choice after so many refusals of others of great worthiness, might be counterprised, or in some manner recompensed.[7]

The Alençon match was allowed to fade, but it revived abruptly in 1579. As always, political and personal circumstances were involved. Alençon had begun to assist the rebels in the Netherlands against Philip II and Elizabeth was eager to support him. He, in turn, required English aid and continued to desire the English crown. His representative Simier appeared at court in January and began ardently to woo the Queen. She was delighted and for a time Alençon's suit prospered, although the Council was divided.

Here Lord Burghley (although he himself inclined toward the match) summarizes the arguments against Alençon. The Queen, it should be added, was now almost 46 years old.

1. Generally for that Monsieur is a Frenchman, the people of this realm naturally hating that nation.

---

[7] From *The Compleat Ambassador,* ed. Dudley Digges (London, 1655), p. 227.

2. Because he is Heir Apparent of France, and by his brother's sickness like to be shortly King of France.

3. If he shall become King, then, if he shall have a son by her Majesty, that son and his posterity male, shall be Kings of France and England, whereby the government of England shall for the most part be under a vice-roy; and if he shall have no son nor daughter, then it is to be doubted that he will hardly leave England to any lawful successor.

4. The doubt that her Majesty either shall not have children, or that she may be endangered in childbirth.

5. The doubt that Monsieur being of a contrary religion, shall be a comfort to all obstinate papists in England and a discomfort to all the subjects of good religion.[8]

> *Alençon himself appeared at court in August. His visit was a secret but everyone knew about it. He was a surprising personal success; if not handsome, he was at least charming, ambitious, and ardent, and the Queen seemed quite swept off her feet.*

. . . The Queen was very angry at the gossip that was going on about Alençon's coming, and she formally ordered that the matter should not be spoken of. Two of her ladies, the Countess of Derby and a daughter of the Earl of Bedford, have been arrested for talking about it, and importance is attached to what the former says, as she and her husband are claimants to the Crown.

They have been lodged in the house of a gentleman in London. The councillors themselves deny that Alençon is here, and in order not to offend the Queen, they shut their eyes and avoid going to Court, so as not to appear to stand in the way of her interviews with him, only attending the Council when they are obliged. It is said that if she marries without consulting her people she may repent it. Leicester is much put out, and all the councillors are disgusted except Sussex, who has led the dance in order, as he says, to upset Leicester and deprive him of French support. The

[8] From *A Collection of State Papers . . . at Hatfield House,* ed. William Murdin (London, 1759), p. 333.

people at large are so displeased, that, if Alencon stays here, they say it is very likely trouble will come of it, above all if they are urged on to it by others. . . .

*   *   *

The Queen is delighted with Alençon, and he with her, as she has let out to some of her courtiers, saying that she was pleased to have known him, was much taken with his good parts, and admired him more than any man. She said that, for her part, she will not prevent his being her husband. The French say the same thing. . . .

Leicester, who is in great grief, came hither recently and when he came from his interview with the Queen, his emotion was remarked. A meeting was held on the same night at the Earl of Pembroke's house, there being present Lord Sidney and other friends and relatives. They no doubt discussed the matter, and some of them afterwards remarked that Parliament would have something to say as to whether the Queen married or not. The people in general seem to threaten revolution about it.

On Sunday the 23rd there was a grand ball where the Queen danced much more than usual, Alençon being placed behind a hanging, and she making signals to him. . . .[9]

The Council was divided and elected to defer to the Queen's wishes. But she was bitter that there were some who had argued against the match. It was becoming apparent that the marriage was politically unwise. The Queen's tears were probably genuine enough; she was watching her last chance of marriage disappear. Here Burghley recounts her reaction.

This message was reported to her Majesty in the forenoon, and she allowed very well of the dutiful offer of their services—nevertheless, she uttered many speeches, and that not without shedding of many tears, that she should find in her councillors, by their long disputations, any disposition to make it doubtful, whether there could be any more surety for her and her realm than to have her

[9] August 22, 25, 1579. From *Calendar of State Papers Spanish Elizabeth* (London, 1894), II, 692–93.

marry, and have a child of her own body to inherit, and so to continue the line of King Henry the VIIIth; and she said she condemned herself of simplicity in committing this matter to be argued by them, for that she thought to have rather had an universal request made to her to proceed in this marriage, than to have made doubt of it; and being much troubled herewith she requested us to forbear her until the afternoon.

In the afternoon we came to know her pleasure, and then she entered to show her great misliking of such as she thought should not prefer her marriage before any device of surety, and with a great number of arguments seemed to reprove them; and because she understood that the doubt of religion, by means of Monsieur's being of a contrary, to be changed or hindered in the realm; she did marvel that any person would think so slenderly for her, as that she would not for God's cause, for herself, for surety, and her people, have so straight regard thereto, as none ought to make that such a doubt, as for it to forbear marriage, and to have the crown settled in her child.[10]

> *The risk of the match was great with the nation divided. By the end of the year, the Queen had made up her mind not to marry. But the situation abroad made it useful to keep up appearances and so the affair continued. Alençon came and went a second time; love letters flowed back and forth across the Channel. But the Queen's heart was no longer in it—if indeed it had ever been. In any case, Alençon's sudden death in 1584 ended the affair once and for all. Elizabeth cried for many days afterward. Were the tears for Alençon, for the passing years, or, as the French ambassador preferred to think, merely for show?*

[10] From *A Collection of State Papers . . . at Hatfield House,* ed. William Murdin (London, 1759), pp. 336–37.

10
The Queen and Mary Stuart

Surely the most fascinating, puzzling, and personal of Elizabeth's problems was her rivalry with Mary Stuart. Here all the other problems of the reign found focus—religion, foreign policy, the succession—now complicated by jealousy and ambition. The literature describing their relationship is enormous and controversial; the two queens have continued to exert their feminine charms through the centuries, dividing their biographers as once they did their followers. Romance and intrigue, farce and tragedy, combine to keep the story alive and endlessly interesting. To tell it simply is impossible; to describe its significance to Elizabeth is all that may be suggested.

Mary was daughter to James V, the King of Scotland. She was also a granddaughter of Henry VII and a cousin of Elizabeth. At her birth in 1542 she was thus a claimant to two crowns. With her betrothal soon afterwards to the dauphin of France, she could hope for a third. She achieved the first as an infant, upon the death of her father. She achieved the last as a young woman, the bride of Francis II. In the meanwhile she was raised and educated among the royal children at the French court. To her natural beauty and charm she added many accomplishments, as well as a strict Roman Catholicism. At Elizabeth's accession she maintained her English claims and refused to recognize Elizabeth's title. But Francis died suddenly in 1560, and Mary was suddenly bereft of both husband and French crown. She hurried home at once to Scotland to claim her remaining title and despite the opposition of a strong Protestant party and the great preacher John Knox, she made good her claim and began to rule. The stage was set at last for a long struggle between two remarkable women.

In 1560 the Treaty of Edinburgh brought the Anglo-Scottish war to a conclusion. French troops were required to withdraw, and Francis and Mary were bound to recognize Elizabeth's title. But although peace was in fact achieved, Mary refused to ratify the last provision. It was not that she thought to replace Elizabeth; she wished rather to strengthen her own bargaining position in the order of succession. Although blood gave her precedence, foreign birth and Catholic faith were strong arguments for her exclusion. But Mary's tactics betrayed her; Elizabeth's suspicions were aroused. The existence of a strong Catholic party in England and her lack of an heir made Mary's actions potentially dangerous. Relations between the queens began thus in stress and suspicion. Although efforts were made to reconcile them—they almost met on several occasions—events invariably conspired to keep them apart.

Elizabeth made an effort at reconciliation in 1563. Mary's marriage plans, like Elizabeth's, were critical. To preserve the peace with Scotland, Elizabeth thought it desirable to see Mary married to an Englishman. What better candidate than her own beloved Leicester! This startling suggestion has baffled many since, but its political advantages were perfectly clear and Elizabeth was quite probably sincere. The Scottish Queen had her own plans, however, and they were beginning to fasten on another but more dangerous English candidate, Henry Stuart, Lord Darnley. His mother was Lady Lennox, another cousin of Elizabeth but ambitious, Catholic, and personally disliked by the Queen. In 1564 Darnley sought permission from Elizabeth to visit his Scottish estates, while at about the same time Mary dispatched a special envoy, Sir James Melville, to Elizabeth to discuss the succession. Afterwards he recalled his visit. As a description of the Queen, with all her accomplishments and vanity, it is, incidentally, one of the most brilliant that we possess.

Being arrived at London, I lodged near the Court which was at Westminster. . . . That same night her Majesty sent Mr. Hatton . . . in her name to welcome me, and to show me, that the next morning she would give me audience in her garden at eight of the clock. . . .

*   *   *

I found her Majesty walking in an alley. And after I had kissed her hand, and presented my letter of credence, I told her Majesty in French the effect of my commission, as near to the aforesaid instructions as I could; and sometimes being interrupted by her demands, I answered as I judged most pertinent. The reason why I spoke French was, that being but lately come home, I could not speak my own language so promptly as was requisite. . . .

* * *

Thus the old friendship being renewed, she inquired if the Queen had sent any answer to the proposition of marriage made to her by Mr. Randolph. I answered, as I had been instructed, that my mistress thought little or nothing thereof, but expected the meeting of some commissioners upon the Borders, with my Lord of Murray and the Secretary Lethington, to confer and treat upon all such matters of greatest importance, as should be judged to concern the quiet of both the countries and satisfaction of both their Majesties' minds . . . and expects that your Majesty will send my Lord of Bedford and my Lord Robert Dudley.

She answered, it appeared that I made but small account of my Lord Robert, seeing that I named the Earl of Bedford before him: but said that ere long she would make him a far greater Earl, and that I should see it done before my returning home. For she esteemed him as her brother and best friend, whom she would have herself married, had she ever minded to have taken a husband. But being determined to end her life in virginity, she wished that the Queen her sister might marry him, as meetest of all other with whom she could find in her heart to declare her second person. For being matched with him, it would best remove out of her mind all fears and suspicions, to be offended by any usurpation before her death. Being assured that he was so loving and trusty, that he would never permit any such thing to be attempted during her time.

And that the Queen my mistress might have the higher esteem of him, I was required to stay till I should see him made Earl of Leicester, and Baron of Denbigh; which was done at Westminster with great solemnity, the Queen herself helping to put on his ceremonial, he sitting upon his knees before her with a great gravity. But she could not refrain from putting her hand in his neck, smilingly tickling him, the French Ambassador and I standing by. Then she turned, asking at me, "How I liked him?" I answered, that as he was a worthy servant, so he was happy who had a princess who could discern and reward good service. Yet, says she, you like better of yonder long lad, pointing towards my Lord Darnley, who as nearest prince of the blood, did bear the sword of honor that day before her. My answer was, that no woman of spirit would make choice of such a man, who more resembled a woman than a man. For he was handsome, beardless and lady-faced. And I had no will that she should think that I liked him, or had any eye or dealing that way. Albeit I had a secret charge to deal with my Lady Lennox, to endeavor to procure liberty for him to go to Scotland (where his father was already) under the pretext of seeing the country, and conveying the Earl his father back again to England.

Now I found the Queen of England was determined to treat with my sovereign, first concerning her marriage with the Earl of Leicester, and for that effect she promised to send commissioners unto the Borders. In the meantime I was very favorably and familiarly used. For during nine days that I remained at the Court, it pleased her Majesty to confer with me every day, and sometimes thrice in a day, in the morning, after dinner and after supper. Sometimes she would say, that seeing she could not meet with the Queen her good sister to confer with her familiarly, that she was resolved to open a good part of her inward mind to me, that I might show it again unto the Queen. She told me she was not so much offended with the Queen's angry letter, as that she seemed so far to disdain the marriage of my Lord of Leicester. . . .

She appeared to be so affectionate to the Queen her good sister, that she expressed a great desire to see her. And because their so much, by her, desired meeting could not be so hastily brought to pass, she appeared with great delight to look upon her Majesty's picture. She took me to her bed-chamber and opened a little cabinet, wherein were divers little pictures wrapt within paper, and their names written with her own hand upon the papers. Upon the first that she took up was written, "My Lord's Picture," I held the candle, and pressed to see that picture so named. She appeared loath to let me see it; yet my importunity prevailed for a sight thereof, and found it to be the Earl of Leicester's picture. I desired that I might have it to carry home to my Queen; which she refused, alleging that she had but that one picture of his. I said, your Majesty hath here the original; for I perceived him at the farthest part of the chamber, speaking with Secretary Cecil. Then she took out the Queen's picture, and kissed it; and I adventured to kiss her hand, for the great love therein evidenced to my mistress. She showed me also a fair ruby, as great as a tennis-ball. I desired that she would either send it, or my Lord Leicester's picture, as a token unto the Queen. She said, if the Queen would follow her counsel, that she would in process of time get all she had; that in the meantime she was resolved in a token to send her with me a fair diamond.

*　　*　　*

At divers meetings we had divers purposes. The Queen my mistress had instructed me to leave matters of gravity sometimes, and cast in merry purposes, lest otherwise I should be wearied, she being well informed of that Queen's natural temper. Therefore, in declaring my observations of the customs of Dutchland, Poland, and Italy, the busking of the woman was not forgot, and what country weed I thought best becoming gentlewomen. The Queen said she had clothes of every sort; which every day thereafter, so long as I was there, she changed. One day she had the English weed, another the French, and another the Italian, and so forth. She asked me which of them became her best. I answered, "In my judgment, the Italian dress": which answer I found pleased her well; for she delighted to show her golden colored hair, wearing a caul and bonnet as they do in Italy. Her hair was more reddish than yellow, curled in appearance naturally. She desired to know of me, what color of hair was reputed best; and whether my Queen's hair or hers was best; and which of the two was fairest. I answered, "The fairest of them both was not their worst faults." But she was earnest with me to declare which of them I judged fairest. I said "She was the fairest Queen in England, and mine the fairest Queen in Scotland." Yet she appeared earnest. I answered, "They were both the fairest ladies in their countries; that her Majesty was whiter, but my Queen was very lovely." She inquired which of them was of highest stature. I said, "My Queen." "Then," saith she, "she is too high; for I myself am neither too high nor too low." Then she asked what kind of exercises she used. I answered, that when I received my dispatch, the Queen was lately come from the Highland hunting: that when her more serious affairs permitted, she was taken up with reading of histories: that sometimes she recreated herself in playing upon the lute and virginals. She asked if she played well. I said, "reasonably for a Queen."

That same day after dinner, my Lord of Hunsdon drew me up to a quiet gallery, that I might hear some music (but he said that he durst not avow it) where I might hear the Queen play upon the virginals. After I had hearkened a while, I took by the tapestry that hung before the door of the chamber, and seeing her back was toward the door, I entered within the chamber, and stood a pretty space hearing her play excellently well. But she left off immediately, so soon as she turned her about and saw me. She appeared to be surprised to see me, and came forward, seeming to strike me with her hand; alleging she used not to play before men, but when she was solitary, to shun melancholy. She asked how I came there. I answered, "As I was walking with my Lord of Hunsdon, as we passed by the chamber-door, I heard such melody as ravished me, whereby I was drawn in ere I knew how; excusing my fault of homeliness, as being brought up in the Court of France, where such freedom was allowed; declaring myself willing to endure what kind of punishment her Majesty should be pleased to inflict upon me for so great an offence." Then she sat down low upon a cushion, and I upon my knees by her; but with her own hand she gave me a cushion, to lay under my knee; which at first I refused, but she compelled me to take it. She then called for my Lady Strafford out of the next chamber; for the Queen was alone. She inquired whether my Queen or she played best. In that I found myself obliged to give her the praise. She said my French was good, and asked if I could speak Italian; which she spoke reasonably well. I told her Majesty I had no time to learn the language perfectly, not having been above two months in Italy. Then she spake to me in Dutch, which was not good; and would know what kind of books I most delighted in, whether theology, history, or love matters. I said, "I liked well of all the sorts." Here I took occasion to press earnestly my dispatch. She said I was weary sooner of her company, than she was of mine. I told her Majesty, that though I had no reason of being weary, I knew my mistress her affairs called me home: yet I was stayed two days longer, till I might see her dance, as I was afterward informed. Which being over, she inquired of me, whether she or my Queen danced best. I answered, "The Queen danced not so high, and disposedly as she did." [1]

> *Mary married Darnley over Elizabeth's objections in 1565 and, to compound the offence, soon gave birth to a son, the future James I. Melville here recalls the Queen's reaction on receiving the news.*

All the while I lay within the Castle of Edinburgh, praying night and day for her Majesty's good and happy delivery of a fair son. This prayer being granted, I was the first who was thereof advertised, by the Lady Boyne, in her Majesty's name, to part with diligence the 19 of June 1566, betwixt ten and eleven in the morning. By twelve of the clock I took horse, and was that night at Berwick. The fourth day after I was at London; and did first meet with my brother Sir Robert, who that same night sent and advertised Secretary Cecil of my arrival, and of the birth of the Prince; desiring him to keep it quiet till my coming to Court, to show it myself unto her Majesty, who was for the time at Greenwich, where her Majesty was in great mirth, dancing after supper. But so soon as the Secretary Cecil whispered in her ear the news of the Prince's birth, all her mirth was laid aside for that night; all present marvelling whence proceeded such a change; for the Queen did sit down, putting her hand under her cheek, bursting out to some of her ladies, that the Queen of Scots was mother of a fair son, while she was but a barren stock. [2]

> *By 1565, Mary had successfully defied her Protestant opposition and the Queen of England. Her real abilities and*

[1] From *Memoirs of Sir James Melville*, ed. A. Francis Steuart (London, 1929), pp. 89–97. Reprinted by permission of Routledge & Kegan Paul Ltd.

[2] From *Memoirs of Sir James Melville*, ed. A. Francis Steuart (London, 1929), pp. 130–31. Reprinted by permission of Routledge & Kegan Paul Ltd.

moderate policies had also won considerable support. But all was swiftly shattered. More than anything else, Mary's affections seem to have betrayed her. It is usual to portray the rival queens in perfect contrast. Nowhere is this so obvious as in the way Mary allowed her emotions to overwhelm her reason and policy. Within a year she had fallen out with Darnley, who proved to be a thoroughly objectionable person —vain, weak and incapable. She turned to an Italian named Rizzio to conduct her business, but he too offended everyone. Rizzio was promptly murdered by a conspiracy of noblemen, including the jealous Darnley. Mary's estrangement from Darnley was now complete, and she turned her affections on a wild Scottish nobleman, the Earl of Bothwell. So far scandal had been circumscribed; now it exploded—literally. The house to which Darnley had been lured by Mary was blown to pieces. This was followed almost immediately by the marriage of Mary to Bothwell and a mock trial exonerating the latter.

At news of Darnley's death, Elizabeth hastily dispatched a letter to Mary.

Madame. My ears have been so astounded and my heart so frightened to hear of the horrible and abominable murder of your husband and my cousin that I have scarcely spirit to write: yet I cannot conceal that I grieve more for you than him. I should not do the office of a faithful cousin and friend, if I did not urge you to preserve your honor, rather than look through your fingers at revenge on those who have done you "such pleasure" as most people say. I counsel you so to take this matter to heart, that you may show the world what a noble princess and loyal woman you are. I write thus vehemently not that I doubt, but for affection. As for the three matters communicated by Melville, I understand your wish to please me, and that you will grant the request by Lord Bedford in my name to ratify the treaty made 6 or 7 years past. On other things I will not trouble you at length, referring you to the report of this gentleman.[3]

[3] February 24, 1567 (from French). From *Calendar of State Papers Scottish 1563–69* (London, 1900), p. 316.

At the news of Mary's marriage, Elizabeth wrote again.

Madame: It has been always held in friendship "that prosperity provideth, but adversity proveth friends," wherefore we comfort you with these few words. We understand by your trusty servant Robert Melville of your estate, and as much as could be said for your marriage. To be plain with you, our grief has not been small thereat: for how could a worse choice be made for your honor than in such haste to marry such a subject who, besides other notorious lacks, public fame has charged with the murder of your late husband, besides touching yourself in some part, though we trust in that behalf, falsely. And with what peril have you married him, that hath another lawful wife alive, whereby neither by God's law nor man's, yourself can be his lawful wife nor any children betwixt you legitimate?

Thus you see our opinion plainly, and we are heartily sorry we can conceive no better, what colorable reasons soever we have heard of your servant to induce us otherwise. We are earnestly bent to do everything in our power to procure the punishment of that murder against any subject you have, how dear you should hold him, and next thereto, to be careful how your son the prince may be preserved to the comfort of you and your realm.

For your comfort in such your present adversity, as we hear you are in, we are determined to do all in our power for your honor and safety, and to send with all speed one of our trusty servants not only to understand your state, but thereon so to deal with your nobility and people, as they shall find you not to lack our friendship and power.[4]

But the marriage was Mary's undoing. It led eventually to rebellion, imprisonment, defeat, and escape—fatefully—to England. The infant James in the meanwhile was pronounced

[4] June 23, 1675. From *Calendar of State Papers Scottish* 1563–69 (London, 1900), pp. 336–37.

King of Scotland. The question for Elizabeth—what to do with her captive—was to plague her for almost 20 years. Sir Francis Knollys explains the problem in a letter to Cecil from Carlisle where Mary was first held.

And yet this lady and princess is a notable woman. She seemeth to regard no ceremonious honor beside the acknowledging of her estate regal. She showeth a disposition to speak much, to be bold, to be pleasant, and to be very familiar. She showeth a great desire to be avenged of her enemies. She showeth a readinss to expose herself to all perils in hope of victory. She delighteth much to hear of hardiness and valiancy; commending by name all approved hardy men of her country although they be her enemies; and she concealeth no cowardness even in her friends. The thing that most she thirsteth after is victory, and it seemeth to be indifferent to her to have her enemies diminished either by the sword of her friends, or by the liberal promises and rewards of her purse, or by division and quarrels raised amongst themselves: so that for victory's sake pain and peril seemeth pleasant unto her. And in respect of victory, wealth and all things seemeth to her contemptuous and vile. Now what is to be done with such a lady and princess, or whether such a princess and lady be to be nourished in one's bosom, or whether it be good to halt and dissemble with such a lady I refer to your judgment.[5]

Elizabeth was of two minds and long remained so. She detested rebellion against princes with all her heart and the Scottish Queen's fallen state aroused her pity and sympathy. But she feared and distrusted Mary as well. At first she worked for her restoration, but Mary was too restless to remain quietly captive. She soon became the focus for plots directed against Elizabeth. The first to erupt was the Northern Rebellion. It was followed almost at once by a treasonous scheme devised by an Italian named Ridolfi. This time Mary was involved with Philip II, the Pope, and the Duke of Norfolk. When the plot

[5] June 11, 1568. From *Original Letters,* 1st series, ed. Ellis (London, 1824), II, 246.

was discovered, Norfolk was apprehended and tried for treason. The nation was aroused; Parliament and Council clamored for the execution of Norfolk and Mary both. Yet Elizabeth hesitated. Four times warrants of execution were issued against Norfolk; each time she had them stayed. Only with the greatest reluctance did she finally submit. Even then she protected Mary, who remained a prisoner—and a problem —for another 15 years. Here Cecil describes her hesitation to Francis Walsingham.

I cannot write you what is the inward cause of the stay of the Duke of Norfork's death, only I find her Majesty diversely disposed. Sometime when she speaketh of her Majesty's danger, she concludeth that justice should be done; another time when she speaketh of his nearness of blood, of his superiority in honor, etc., she stayeth. As upon Saturday she signed a warrant for the Writs to the Sheriffs of London for his execution on Monday, and so all preparations were made with the expectation of all London, and concourse of many thousands yesterday in the morning; but their coming was answered with another ordinary execution of Mather and Berny, for conspiring the Queen's Majesty's death, and of one Rolph, for counterfeiting the Queen's Majesty's hand twice to get concealed lands. And the cause of this disappointment was this, suddenly on Sunday late in the night, the Queen's Majesty sent for me, and entered into a great misliking that the Duke should die the next day, and said she was and should be disquieted, and said she would have a new warrant made that night to the Sheriffs, to forbear until they should hear further; and so they did: God's will be fulfilled, and aid her Majesty to do herself good.[6]

And so the years passed. Mary was closely confined but inevitably restless. Elizabeth continued to treat with the Scots for Mary's restoration. As James grew to manhood a rapprochement between mother and son began to seem possible. In truth, nothing was less likely; the young King was not

[6] February 11, 1572. From *The Compleat Ambassador,* ed. Dudley Digges (London, 1655), pp. 165–66.

anxious to share the throne under any circumstances. Mary turned more and more to Philip II and the "Enterprise." Her very existence was a threat to Elizabeth's life. The Queen's feelings are probably well represented by a poem she composed.

The doubt of future foes exiles my present joy,
And wit me warns to shun such snares as threaten mine annoy;
For falsehood now doth flow, and subjects' faith doth ebb,
Which should not be if reason ruled or wisdom weaved the web.
But clouds of joy untried do cloak aspiring minds,
Which turn to rain of late repent by changed course of winds.
The top of hope supposed the root upreared shall be,
And fruitless all their grafted guile, as shortly ye shall see.
The dazzled eyes with pride, with great ambition blinds,
Shall be unsealed by worthy wights whose foresight falsehood finds.
The daughter of debate that discord aye doth sow
Shall reap no gain where former rule till peace hath taught to know.
No foreign banished wight shall anchor in this port;
Our realm brooks not seditious sects, let them elsewhere resort.
My rusty sword through rest shall first his edge employ
To poll their tops that seek such change or gape for future joy.[7]

In 1583, a plot against Elizabeth was discovered involving Mary and the Spanish ambassador, Mendoza. The organizer (Francis Throckmorton) was arrested and executed; Mendoza was deported. In the following year, the Protestant Prince William of Orange was assassinated and an attempt was made against Elizabeth. Tyrannicide had been ruled lawful by the Pope. In this climate of fear, Mary's confinement was closer than ever; her mail was secretly monitored. A last conspiracy was soon discovered, this time directed by a man named Babington. Letters were deciphered proving Mary's complicity beyond question. Once again the conspirators were executed, and once again Elizabeth hesitated. Mary was tried by a commission, and Council and Parliament again demanded her

[7] From George Puttenham, *The Arte of English Poesie,* ed. Edward Arber (London, 1869), pp. 255–56.

*execution. No doubt many conflicting thoughts passed through
Elizabeth's mind as she considered Mary's fate. Here Camden
describes her decision.*

Yet she, being a woman naturally slow in her resolutions,
began to consider in her mind, whether it were better to put her
to death, or to spare her. As for putting her to death these things
were against it: her own innate clemency, lest she should seem to
show herself cruel to a woman, and that a princess, and her kinswoman; fear of infamy with posterity in after histories; and im-
minent and certain dangers as well from the King of Scots, who
would now be advanced a step higher in his hopes of England, as
from the Catholic princes and desperate men, who would now
adventure upon anything. And if she should spare her, she foresaw
that no less danger threatened her. The noblemen that had given
sentence against the Queen of Scots would endeavor underhand to
get into favor with her and her son, not without manifest hazard
to herself; the rest of her subjects, who had been so careful for
her safety, seeing she had frustrated their pains and care, would
take it very ill, and for time to come neglect her preservation; many
would turn papists, and entertain greater hopes, when they should
see her preserved as it were by fate to a probability of enjoying the
crown; the Jesuits and seminaries, whose eyes are upon her only,
seeing her sickly, and fearing that she would not live long, would
leave no means untried to hasten Queen Elizabeth's death, that so
their religion might be restored.

The courtiers also continually suggested unto her these things
following, and the like: "Why should you spare her, when she is
guilty and justly condemned, who, though she subscribed to the
Association for your safety, yet presently after, resolved unmerci-
fully to ruin you who were altogether innocent, and by destroying
you to destroy religion, the nobility and people? Clemency and
mercy is a royal virtue, but not to be extended to the merciless.
Let the vain show of mercy give place to wholesome severity. Have
a care that your unseasonable mercy and favor involve you not in
the greatest misery. It is commendation enough of your clemency,
to have spared her once: to spare her again were nothing else but to

pronounce her guiltless, condemn the estates of the realm of injustice, encourage her favorers to hasten their wicked designs, and discourage your faithful subjects from caring for the commonwealth. Religion, the commonwealth, your own safety, the love of your country, the Oath of Association and the care of posterity, do all with their joint prayers beseech you, that she which endangereth the subversion of all these may forthwith be put to death: and except they may prevail, safety itself will never be able to save this commonwealth; and historians will leave it recorded to succeeding ages, that the bright sunshining and glorious days of England under Queen Elizabeth ended in a foul, cloudy and dark evening, yea in an eternal night . . ." which so troubled and staggered the Queen's mind, that she gave herself wholly over to solitariness, sat many times melancholic and mute, and frequently sighing muttered this to herself, *Aut fer, aut feri*, that is, Either bear with her, or smite her, and, out of I know not what emblem, *Ne feriare, feri*, that is, Strike, lest thou be stricken. . . .[8]

On February 8, 1587 Mary was executed. Elizabeth declared that she had never meant to dispatch the death warrant and threw all the blame upon Secretary Davison—as Camden's account suggests. Undoubtedly she feared the foreign reaction, from the French and Scots, as well as from Spain. No doubt too, the horror of the deed sincerely affected her; she had tried to avert it for so long. In any case Davison was fined and imprisoned although he was released upon the defeat of the Armada and his fine apparently remitted. James was satisfied with Elizabeth's apology for the "error." That no accident was involved is apparent from Davison's own explanation of events. In it, he also recounts Elizabeth's desire to have Mary quietly eliminated so that she could avoid the responsibility. Under the Bond of Association (a pact signed by many of her nobility, swearing vengeance on anyone who conspired against the Queen), she might well have hoped for such an expedient. But Sir Amias Paulet, Mary's guardian, was not anxious to accept the burden either. Here is Davison's account.

[8] From William Camden, *The History of Elizabeth*, 3rd ed. (London, 1675), pp. 380–82.

After that the sentence against the Scottish Queen was passed, and subscribed by the lords and others the Commissioners appointed to her trial, and that her Majesty had notified the same to the world by her proclamation according to the statute, there remained nothing but her warrant under the Great Seal of England, for the performing and accomplishing of her execution, which after some instance as well of the Lord and Commons of the whole Parliament then assembled, as of others of her Council and best affected subjects, it pleased her Majesty at length to yield unto, and thereupon gave order to my Lord Treasurer to project the same, which he accordingly performed, and with her Majesty's privity left in my hands to procure her signature. But by reason of the presence of the French and Scottish ambassadors, then suitors for her life, she forebore the signing thereof till the first of February, which was some few days after their departure home. . . . At my coming in, her Highness first demanding of me whither I had been abroad that fair morning, advising me to use [do] it oftener, and reprehending me for the neglect thereof, with other like gracious speeches, arguing a care of my health, finally asked of me what I had in my hands? I answered, divers warrants and other things to be signed that concerned her service. She enquired whether my Lord Admiral had not given me order to bring up the warrant for the Scottish Queen's execution? I answered yes; and, thereupon, asking me for it, I delivered it into her hands, after the reading whereof, she, calling for pen and ink, signed it, and laying it from her, demanded of me whether I were not heartily sorry to see it done? . . . Her Highness . . . passed from the matter to ask me what else I had to sign, and, thereupon, offering unto her some other warrants and instructions touching her service, it pleased her, with the best disposition and willingness that might be, to dispatch them all. After this she commanded me to carry it to the Seal, and to give my Lord Chancellor special order from her to use it as secretly as might be, lest the divulging thereof before the execution might, as she pretended, increase her danger. And in my way to my Lord Chancellor her pleasure also was, that I should visit Mr. Secretary Walsingham, being then sick at his house in London, and communicate the matter with him, because the grief thereof would go near (as she merrily said) to kill him outright, where, taking occasion to repeat unto me some reasons why she had deferred the matter so long, as namely, for her honor's sake, that the world might see that she had not been violently or maliciously drawn thereto, she concluded that she never was so ill advised as not to see and apprehend her own danger, and the necessity she had to proceed to this execution. And thereupon (after some intermingled speech to and fro), told me that she would have it done as secretly as might be, appointing the hall where she was for the place of execution; and misliking the court, or green of the castle for divers respects, she alleged with other speech to like effect. Howbeit, as I was ready to depart, she fell into some complaint of Sir Amias Paulet and others, that might have eased her of this burden, wishing that Mr. Secretary and I would yet write unto both him and Sir Drue Drury, to sound their disposition in that behalf. And albeit I had before excused myself from meddling therein, upon sundry her Majesty's former motions, as a matter I utterly prejudged, assuring her that it should be so much labor lost; knowing the wisdom and integrity of the gentlemen whom I thought would not do so unlawful an act for any respect in the world; yet finding her desirous to have the matter attempted, I promised for her satisfying to signify this her pleasure to Mr. Secretary, and so for that time leaving her, went down directly to my Lord Treasurer, to whom I did communicate the said warrant signed, together with such other particulars as had passed at that time betwixt her Highness and me. The same afternoon I waited on my Lord Chancellor for the sealing of the said warrant, according to her Majesty's direction, which was done between the hours of four and five, from whence I returned back unto Mr. Secretary Walsingham, whom I had visited by the way, and acquainted with her pleasure, touching letters that were to be written to the said Sir Amias Paulet and Sir Drue Drury, which at my return I found ready to be sent away. The next morning about ten of the clock, being in London, Mr. William Killigrew came unto me from her Majesty with this message, that if I had not been with my Lord Chancellor, I should forbear to go unto him till I had spoken again with herself; but that message coming out of season, I returned him back with this general answer, that I would be at the Court as soon as himself, and give her Majesty an account what I had done. At my coming to her, she demanded of me whether the warrant were passed the seal? I told her yes. She asked what needeth that haste? I answered, that I had therein made no more haste than herself commanded, and my duty in a case of that moment required, which as I take it was not to be dallied with. But me thinketh, saith she, that it might have been otherwise handled for the form, naming unto me some that were of that opinion whose judgments she commended. I answered, that I took the honorable and just way to be the safest and best way, if they meant to have it done at all; whereto her Majesty replying nothing, for that time left me and went to dinner. From her I went down to Mr. Vice-chamberlain, with whom I did communicate the said warrant, and other particulars that had passed betwixt her Highness and me, touching the dispatch thereof, where, falling into a rehearsal of some doubtful speeches of hers, betraying a disposition to throw the burden from herself, if by any means she might, and remembering unto him the example of her dealing in the case of the Duke of Norfork's execution, which she had laid heavily upon my Lord Treasurer for a long time after; and how much her disavowing of this justice was more to be feared, considering the timorousness of her sex and nature, the quality of the person who it concerned, and respect of her friends, with many other circumstances that might further and incline her thereunto, I finally told him that I was for mine own part fully resolved, notwithstanding the directions that I had received, to do nothing that might give her any advantage to cast a burden of so great weight upon my single and weak shoulders; and, therefore, having done as much as belonged to my part, would leave to him and others as deeply interested in the surety of her Majesty and the state as myself, to advise what course should now be taken for accomplishing the rest, who, as near as I remember, gave me this answer, that, as he was heartily glad the matter was brought thus far, so did he for his own part wish him hanged that would not join with me in the furtherance thereof; being a cause so much importing the common safety and tranquillity of her Majesty and the whole realm. And so, after some little speech, resolved to go together to my Lord Treasurer to confer thereof with his Lordship, as we immediately

did, and there agreed for the better and more honorable proceeding
therein, to break the matter with the Lords and others of her
Majesty's Council. . . . They finally resolved to proceed to the
sending down thereof without troubling her Highness any further
withal, as well in regard of her charge given to myself, to let her
hear no more thereof till it was done, having otherwise performed
as much as in any reason or law would be required of her, as is
before remembered, as the dangerous consequence might else have
grown thereof in case her Majesty, upon such a needless motion,
should have fallen into any new conceit of interrupting and staying
the course of justice. . . .

The next morning her Majesty being in some speech with Mr.
Ralegh in the private chamber, seeing me come in, called me to her,
and (as if she had understood nothing of these proceedings), smiling,
told me how she had been troubled that night upon a dream she
had, that the Scottish Queen was executed, pretending to have been
so greatly moved with the news against myself, as in that passion
she could have done I wot not what; but this being in a pleasant
and smiling manner, I answered her Majesty, that it was good for
me I was not near her so long as that humor lasted. But withal,
taking hold of her speech, asked her in great earnest what it meant,
and whether, having proceeded thus far, she had not a full and
resolute meaning to go through with the said execution according
to her warrant. Her answer was yes, confirmed with a solemn oath
in some vehemency; this only, she thought that it might have
received a better form, because this threw the whole burden upon
herself; whereto I replied, that the form prescribed by the warrant
was such as the law required, and could not well be altered with
any honesty, justice, or surety of those that were commissioners
therein; neither did I know who could sustain this burden if she
took it not upon her, being Sovereign Magistrate, to whom the
sword was committed of God for the punishment of the wicked,
and defence of the good, and without whose authority, the life or
member of the poorest wretch in her kingdom could not be touched.
She answered, that there were wiser men than myself of other
opinion. I told her I could not answer for other men, yet this I
was sure of, that I had never yet heard any man give a sound
reason to prove it either honorable or safe for her Majesty to take

any other course than that which standeth with law and justice, and so, without further replication or speech, we parted. The same afternoon (as I take it) she asked me whether I had heard from Sir Amias Paulet, I told her no; but within an hour or two after going to London I met with letters from him, in answer to those that were written unto him some few days before, upon her commandment. The next morning, having access unto her Majesty upon some other occasion, I told her of the receipt of them, which her Highness, desirous to see, took and read; but finding thereby that he was grieved with the motion made unto him, offering his life and all he had to be disposed at her pleasure, but absolutely refusing to be an instrument in any such action as was not warranted in honor and justice; her Majesty, falling into terms of offence, complaining of the daintiness and (as she called it) perjury of him and others, who, contrary to their Oath of Association, did cast the burden upon herself, she rose up, and after a turn or two went into the gallery, whither I followed her, and there renewing her former speech, blaming the niceness of those precise fellows (as she termed them), who in words would do great things for her surety, but in deed perform nothing, concluded that she could have well enough done without them. And here, entering into particularities, named unto me (as I remember) one Wingfield, who, she assured me, would, with some others, undertake it; which gave me occasion to show unto her Majesty how dishonorable (in my poor opinion) any such course would be, and how far from preventing the malice and danger which she so much sought to avoid. And so, falling into the particular case of Sir Amias Paulet and Sir Drue Drury, discoursed unto her the great extremity she would have exposed those poor gentlemen to, for if, in a tender care of her surety, they should have done that she desired, she must either allow their act or disallow it; if she allowed it she took the matter upon herself, with her infinite peril and dishonor; if she disallowed it she should not only overthrow the gentlemen themselves, who had always truly and faithfully honored and served her, but also their estates and posterities, besides the dishonor and injustice of such a course, which I humbly besought her Majesty to consider of: and so, after some little digression and speech of Mr. Secretary and others, touching some things passed heretofore, her Majesty, understanding it was time to go to the closet, rose up, and left me. . . . The next (Thursday) morning early, being, as I take it, the day before my coming from Court, my Lord Treasurer sent for me and acquainted me with the news he had received by Henry Talbot of the said Scottish Queen's execution, which (upon some conference had thereof with Mr. Vice-chamberlain and others) he thought it not fit to break suddenly to her Majesty, and therefore concealed it from her all that day; which being nevertheless brought unto her that evening by other means, she would not at the first seem to take knowledge of it, but the next morning, falling into some heat and passion about it, sent for Mr. Vice-chamberlain, to whom she disavowed the said execution as a thing she never commanded or intended, casting the burden generally upon them all, but chiefly upon my shoulders, because (as she pretended) I had, in suffering it to go out of my hands, abused the trust she reposed in me. . . . I returned home, where the next news I heard was that her Majesty had resolved to commit me to the Tower. . . .[9]

[9] From Nicholas H. Nicolas, *Life of William Davison* (London, 1823), Appendix A, pp. 231–49.

11

The Queen and Parliament

The ultimate test of the Queen's ability arose unexpectedly in her parliaments. Traditionally, they were an extraordinary part of the constitution, meeting only irregularly and confining themselves largely to government business, to the passage of new laws and taxes. Not that they were always submissive; as recently as Mary Tudor's reign they had resisted the royal will on a number of occasions. But the sixteenth century Parliament was a body with few privileges, little continuity, and ill-defined procedures. It was called and dismissed at the royal pleasure, and was expected to be submissive to the royal prerogative. That exclusive power extended to all the great matters of state, including religion, the succession, and foreign policy, as well as to the royal administration. Even Parliament's claims to freedom of speech and control over its own membership were recent and limited. Acquiescence was the rule; opposition the exception. Although precedents might be—and were—recited to lay claims for parliamentary power or privilege, only a later misreading of history would extend those claims very far.

Until recently, historians believed that Elizabeth's parliaments had followed the rule. In 44 years, after all, they had assembled but ten times for but 13 sessions. Never did a sitting last as long as 15 weeks, and one indeed met for only four. Several years elapsed between each Parliament, and the sum of their accomplishments seemed slight. Only the last session of 1601 appeared exceptional with its great debate on monopolies, a forecast of things to come, of a growing constitutional crisis. But now, thanks largely to the work of Sir John Neale, we know better: the last Parliament was not exceptional; in some respects it was less recalcitrant than earlier ones. It was lack of information, not lack of opposition that had made them seem submissive. Now new sources and the reinterpretation of older ones has revealed a long series of encounters between Elizabeth and her Parliaments that continuously tested her power and her abilities.

The difference was in the House of Commons. Long subordinate to the Lords, the lower house had been turned into the representative of the real wealth and political power of England by the gradual social transformation of the sixteenth century. The House of Commons represented the new gentry and merchant classes, and it grew steadily in size, in prestige, and in self-confidence. Many of the great Elizabethans joined its ranks, Bacon, Ralegh, Drake, Cecil, and the rest. And it became the locus of Puritan sentiment, a religious viewpoint not easily overawed or submissive.

Elizabeth's relations with her Parliaments have been described then as a series of contests, not so much between rivals as between two strong personalities, each confident of knowing and representing the national interest, each respectful and indeed affectionate toward the other. Although their wills clashed often, their mutual admiration remained undiminished. Elizabeth never allowed jealousy of the prerogative to alienate her subjects, and in their keenest disappointments the Commons never did grow angry at her. Her consummate political skill, now firm, now yielding, always tactful and appealing, always pragmatic, produced its appropriate result. The Queen almost always had her way.

Of all her roles, the Queen in Parliament may well have been Elizabeth's most brilliant.

We have seen the importance of the problem of the succession. To the Parliament assembled in 1559, as to subsequent assemblies, nothing seemed as important as securing a Protestant heir. Among its first actions, then, was a petition to the Queen to marry. Her reply was read to the House of Commons.

As I have good cause, so do I give you all my hearty thanks, for the good zeal and loving care you seem to have, as well towards me, as to the whole estate of your country. Your petition I perceive consisteth of three parts, and my answer to the same shall depend of two.

And to the first part, I may say unto you, that from my years of understanding, since I first had consideration of myself to be born a servant of Almighty God, I happily chose this kind of life, in the which I yet live. . . .

For the other part, the manner of your petition I do well like, and take it in good part, because it is simple, and containeth no limitation of place or person. If it had been otherwise, I must needs have misliked it very much, and thought it in you a very great presumption, being unfitting and altogether unmete for you to require them, that may command; or those to appoint whose parts are to desire, or such to bind and limit, whose duties are to obey, or to take upon you to draw my love to your liking, or to frame my will to your fantasy: for a guerdon constrained, and gift freely given, can never agree together. Nevertheless, if any of you be in suspect, whensoever it may please God to incline my heart to another kind of life, you may very well assure yourselves, my meaning is not to determine anything, wherewith the realm may or shall have just cause to be discontented. And therefore put that clean out of your heads. For I assure you (what credit my assurance may have with you, I cannot tell, but what credit it shall deserve to have, the sequel shall declare) I will never in that matter conclude anything that shall be prejudicial to the realm. For the well, good and safety whereof, I will never shun to spend my life, and whomsoever my chance shall be to light upon, I trust he shall be such, as shall be as careful for the realm, as you; I will not say as myself, because I cannot so certainly determine of any other, but by my desire he shall be such as shall be as careful for the preservation of the realm and you, as myself. And albeit it might please Almighty God to continue me still in this mind, to live out of the state of marriage, yet is it not to be feared but he will so work in my heart, and in your wisdom, as good provision by his help may be made, whereby the realm shall not remain destitute of an heir that may be a fit governor, and peradventure more beneficial to the realm than such off-spring as may come of me. For though I be never so careful of your well doing, and mind ever so to be, yet may my issue grow

out of kind, and become perhaps ungracious, and in the end, this
shall be for me sufficient, that a marble stone shall declare, that a
Queen having reigned such a time, lived and died a virgin. . . .[1]

*In 1563 and in 1566 new petitions were presented. This
time more stubborn tactics were devised by the radical Protestant group that had collected about the Marian exiles. The
succession question was now attached to a subsidy bill, making
the Queen dependent for supplies on submitting to parliamentary desires. Elizabeth was furious, as a hastily scribbled
note to Burghley suggests.*

Let these two concernings into one meaning, and my counsel
is all given; let not others regard themselves so holy as I have no
corner left for me. Let them know that I knew, though I followed
not, that some of them would my pure conscience better served
me than their lewd practises could avail with me. I know no reason
why any my private answers to the realm should serve for prologue
to a subsidy vote; neither yet do I understand why such audacity
should be used to make without my licence an Act of my words;
are my words like lawyers books which now a days go to the wire-
drawers to make subtle doings more plain? Is there no hold of my
speech without an Act compel me to confirm? Shall my princely
consent be turned to strengthen my words that be not of themselves
substantives? Say no more at this time, but if these fellows were
well answered and paid with lawful coin there would be fewer
counterfeits among them.[2]

*At the same time, various Puritan reform measures were also
introduced into the House of Commons. The Queen defended
her prerogative and refused to yield either on the the matter of
marriage or religion. This in turn raised the question of Parliament's right to freedom of speech. On the last day of the*

---

[1] From Sir Simonds D'Ewes, *The Journals of all the Parliaments of Elizabeth*
(London, 1682), pp. 46–47.
[2] From *Original Letters*, ed. Ellis (London, 1824), I, ii, 226.

session, Elizabeth reprimanded Parliament herself. Very little had been accomplished by the quarrelsome assembly.

My Lords, and others the Commons of this Assembly. Although the Lord Keeper hath, according to order very well answered in my name, yet as a periphrasis I have a few words further to speak unto you: notwithstanding I have not been used nor love to do it, in such open assemblies. Yet now (not to the end to amend his talk) but remembering, that commonly prince's own words be better printed in the hearer's memory, than those spoken by her command, I mean to say thus much unto you. I have in this Assembly found so much dissimulation, where I always professed plainness, that I marvel thereat, yea two faces under one hood, and the body rotten, being covered with two vizors, succession and liberty, which they determined must be either presently granted, denied or deferred. In granting whereof, they had their desires, and denying or deferring thereof (those things being so plaudable, as indeed to all men they are) they thought to work me that mischief, which never foreign enemy could bring to pass, which is the hatred of my Commons. But alas they began to pierce the vessel before the wine was fined, and began a thing not foreseeing the end, how by this means I have seen my well-willers from mine enemies, and can, as me seemeth, very well divide the House into four.

First the broachers and workers thereof, who are in the greatest fault. Secondly, the speakers, who by eloquent tales persuaded others, are in the next degree. Thirdly, the agreers, who being so light of credit, that the eloquence of the tales so overcame them, that they gave more credit thereunto, than unto their own wits. And lastly, those that sat still mute, and meddled not therewith, but rather wondered disallowing the matter; who in my opinion, are most to be excused.

But do you think, that either I am unmindful of your surety by succession, wherein is all my care, considering I know myself to be mortal? No, I warrant you: Or that I went about to break your liberties? No, it was never in my meaning, but to stay you before you fell into the ditch. For all things have their time. And although perhaps you may have after me one better learned, or wiser; yet I assure you, none more careful over you. And, therefore, henceforth, whether I live to see the like Assembly or no, or whoever it be, yet beware however you prove your Prince's patience, as you have now done mine. And now to conclude, all this notwithstanding (not meaning to make a Lent of Christmas) the most part of you may assure yourselves, that you depart in your Prince's grace.[3]

The Queen could always veto bills, but she preferred often to quash them while they were still under consideration. This she could do by sending word to Parliament that her prerogative was being endangered or, ultimately, by imprisoning the offending members. When Parliament was assembled in 1571, the Lord Keeper warned that it "should do well to meddle with no matters of state but such as should be proposed unto them." When the Puritans introduced religious legislation that would have entirely reorganized the church, the Queen vetoed the bills and detained at least one recalcitrant member. In 1572, a new Parliament petitioned Elizabeth for Mary Stuart's execution and again passed some Puritan legislation, once more provoking messages and vetoes. At length the Queen's interference was challenged by the Puritans. In 1576, Peter Wentworth made a great speech enlarging on the privileges of the House of Commons. The issue was plainly drawn: parliamentary privilege vs. the prerogative of the Crown. Wentworth was ordered to the Tower but was released soon afterward. It was but the beginning of his stormy career.

Mr. Speaker, I find written in a little volume these words in effect: Sweet is the name of liberty, but the thing itself a value beyond all inestimable treasure. So much more it behooveth us to take care lest we contenting ourselves with the sweetness of the name, lose and forgo the thing, being of the greatest value that can come unto this noble realm. The inestimable treasure is the use of it in this House. . . . I was never of Parliament but the last and the last session, at both which times I saw the liberty of free speech, the which is the only salve to heal all the sores of this common-

[3] From Sir Simonds D'Ewes, *The Journals of All the Parliaments of Elizabeth* (London, 1682), pp. 116–17.

wealth, so much and so many ways infringed, and so many abuses offered to this honorable council, as hath much grieved me even of very conscience and love to my prince and state . . .

* * *

Amongst others, Mr. Speaker, two things do great hurt in this place, of the which I do mean to speak: the one is a rumor which runneth about the House and this it is, take heed what you do, the Queen's Majesty liketh not such a matter, whosoever prefereth it, she will be offended with him; or the contrary, her Majesty liketh of such a matter, whosoever speaketh against it she will be much offended with him.

The other: sometimes a message is brought into the House, either of commanding or inhibiting, very injurious to the freedom of speech and consultation. I would to God, Mr. Speaker, that these two were buried in hell, I mean rumors and messages; for wicked undoubtedly they are. The reason is, the devil was the first author of them, from whom proceedeth nothing but wickedness. . . .[4]

The Queen was particularly proud of her parliamentary speeches. When she concluded the 1576 session with a highly rhetorical performance (too long and too rhetorical for inclusion here) she sent a copy to John Harington, then only 14 years old, with these words.

Boy Jack, I have made a clerk write fair my poor words for thine use, as it cannot be such striplings have entrance into parliament assembly as yet. Ponder them in thy hours of leisure, and play with them till they enter thine understanding; so shalt thou hereafter, perchance, find some good fruits hereof when thy Godmother is out of remembrance. And I do this because thy father was ready to serve and to love us in trouble and thrall.[5]

[4] From Sir Simonds D'Ewes, *The Journals of All the Parliaments of Elizabeth* (London, 1682), pp. 236–39.
[5] From *Nugae Antiquae*, ed. Thomas Park (London, 1804), p. 127.

The 1586–1587 Parliament renewed its petitions for Mary Stuart's execution; the setting now was the Babington plot. Twice Elizabeth replied. Here is part of her second speech. It was published afterward as The Copie of a Letter to . . . Leycester, *apparently in a version reworked by the Queen herself, although without acknowledgment.*

When first I took the scepter, my title made me not forget the Giver: and therefore began, as it became me, with such religion, as both I was born in, bred in, and I trust shall die in. Although I was not so simple, as not to know what danger and peril so great an alteration might procure me; how many great princes of the contrary opinion would attempt all they might against me; and generally what enmity I should breed unto myself; which all I regarded not, knowing that He, for whose sake I did it, might, and would defend me. For which it is, that ever since I have been so dangerously prosecuted, as I rather marvel that I am, then muse that I should not be; if it were not God's holy hand that continueth me, beyond all other expectation.

Then entered I further into the school of experience, bethinking what it fitted a king to do: and there I saw, he scant was well furnished, if either he lacked justice, temperance, magnanimity, or judgment. As for the two latter, I will not boast, my sex doth not permit it: but for the two first, this dare I say, amongst my subjects I never knew a difference of person, where right was one; nor never to my knowledge preferred for favor, whom I thought not fit for worth; nor bent my ears to credit a tale that first was told me; nor was so rash, to corrupt my judgment with my censure, before I heard the cause. I will not say, but many reports might fortune be brought me by such as might hear the case, whose partiality might mar sometime the matter: for we princes may not hear all ourselves. But this dare I boldly afirm, my verdict went ever with the truth of my knowledge. As full well wished Alcibiades' friend, that he should not give any answer, till he had recited the letters of the alphabet: so have I not used over-sudden resolutions, in matters that have touched me full near: you will say that with me, I think.

And therefore as touching your counsels and consultations, I conceive them to be wise, honest, and conscionable; so provident and careful for the safety of my life (which I wish no longer than may be for your good), that though I never can yield you of recompense your due: yet shall I endeavor myself to give you cause, to think your good will not ill bestowed, and strive to make myself worthy for such subjects.

And now for your petition. I shall pray you for this present, to content yourselves with an answer without answer: your judgment I condemn not, neither do I mistake your reasons, but pray you to accept my thankfulness, excuse my doubtfulness, and take in good part my answer answerless: wherein I attribute not so much to mine own judgment, but that I think many particular persons may go before me, though by my degree I go before them. Therefore if I should say, I would not do what you request, it might peradventure be more than I thought: and to say I would do it, might perhaps breed peril of that you labor to preserve, being more than in our own wisdoms and discretions would seem convenient, circumstances of place and time being duly considered.[6]

Elizabeth's last two Parliaments were marked by economic agitation and opposition. There were many causes of unrest, plague and crop failure, as well as government policy. In 1597–1598, Parliament debated the subsidy with more acrimony than usual, and also raised the question of monopolies. These were royal patents granting exclusive privileges for inventions, processes, exports, etc.; and they were useful as revenue devices. But they were much hated and the Queen promised reforms. Little had been accomplished by 1601, however, and a great new debate began. Although the matter touched clearly upon her prerogative, the Queen saw, as she had often before, that principle was less important than policy. She conceded at once, using all her skill and diplomacy, and won the heartfelt thanks of Parliament and people. It was one of her greatest moments. A diarist records (1) the message from

[6] From *Somers Tracts*, ed. W. Scott (London, 1809), pp. 234–36.

the Queen, (2) the gratitude of the Commons, and (3) the Queen's own speech. The latter was swiftly published—again in a recension by the Queen—and became known as the "Golden Speech."

(1) Mr. Speaker, after a silence (and everyone marveling why the Speaker stood up) spake to this effect:

It pleased her Majesty to command me to attend upon her yesterday in the afternoon, from whom, I am to deliver unto you all, her Majesty's most gracious message, sent by my unworthy self.

She yieldeth you all hearty thanks, for your care, and special regard of those things that concern her state and kingdom, and consequently ourselves; whose good she hath always tendered as her own: for our speedy resolution in making so hasty and free a subsidy; which commonly succeeded and never went before our councils.

For our loyalty, I will assure you, with such and so great zeal of affection she uttered, and showed the same, that to express it with our tongues we are not able, neither our hearts to conceive it. It pleased her Majesty to say unto me, that if she had an hundred tongues, she could not express our hearty good wills; and further, she said, that as she had ever held our good, most dear; so the last day of ours, or her life, should witness it. And that if the least of her subjects were grieved, and herself not touched, she appealed to the throne of Almighty God; how careful she hath been, and will be to defend her people from all oppression.

She said, that partly by intimation of her Council, and partly by divers petitions that have been delivered unto her, both going to Chapel, and also walking abroad; she understood, that divers patents that she had granted, were grievous unto her subjects, and that the substitutes of the patentees had used great oppression. But, she said, she never assented to grant anything that was *malum in se* [bad in itself]. And if in the abuse of her grant, there be anything that is evil, which she took knowledge there was, she, herself, would take present order for reformation thereof.

I cannot express unto you, the apparent indignation of her Majesty, towards these abuses. She said, her kingly prerogative was

tender, and therefore desireth us not to speak or doubt of her careful reformation. For, she said, her commandment given a little before the late troubles (meaning the Earl of Essex's matters) by the
unfortunate event of them, was not so hindered, but that since that
time, even in the midst of her most weighty and great occasions, she
thought upon them. And that this should not suffice, but that
further order should be taken presently, and not *in futuro*. (For
that also was a word which I take it, her Majesty used) and that
some should presently be repealed, some suspended, and not put
in execution: but such as should first have a trial according to the
law, for the good of her people.

Against the abuses, her wrath was so incensed, that, she said, she
neither would, nor could suffer such to escape with impunity.

So to my unspeakable comfort, she hath made me the messenger
of this her gracious thankfulness, and care.

Now we see, that the ax of her princely justice is put to the root
of the tree. And so we see her gracious goodness hath prevented
our councils, and consultations; for which God make us thankful,
and send her long, and long to reign amongst us.

(2) Mr. Francis Moore said: "I must confess, Mr. Speaker, I
moved the House both the last Parliament, and this, touching this
point; but I never meant (and I hope, this House thinketh so) to
set limits and bounds to the prerogative royal."

"But now, seeing it hath pleased her Majesty of herself, out of
the abundance of her princely goodness, to set at liberty her subjects, from the thraldom of these monopolies; from which there
was no city, town, or country free: I would be bold to offer in one
motion, two considerations to the House."

"The first, that Mr. Speaker might go unto her Majesty, to yield
her most humble and hearty thanks; and withal, to show the joy
of her subjects for their delivery, and thankfulness unto her for the
same."

"The other, whereas divers speeches have been made extravagantly in this House, which doubtless have been told her Majesty; and perhaps, all ill conceived of by her: I would therefore,
that Mr. Speaker not only should satisfy her Majesty, by way of
apology therein; but also humbly crave pardon for the same."

Mr. Wingfield said: "My heart is not able to conceive the joy that I feel; and, I assure you, my tongue cannot utter the same. If a sentence of everlasting happiness had been pronounced unto me, it could not have made me show more outward joy, than now I do; which I cannot refrain here to express" (and, as I think, he wept.) There could nothing have been more acceptable to the subject, than this message. And I verily think, that if ever any of her Majesty's words were meritorious before God, I do think these are.

(3) We have heard your declaration, and perceive your care of our state, by falling into the consideration of a greatful acknowledgment of such benefits as you have received; and that your coming is to present thanks unto us, which I accept with no less joy, than your loves can have desire to offer such a present.

I do assure you, there is no prince that loveth his subjects better, of whose love can countervail our love. There is no jewel, be it of never so rich a price, which I set before this jewel; I mean, your love: for I do more esteem of it, than of any treasure or riches; for that we know how to prize, but love and thanks I count unvaluable.

And, though God hath raised me high; yet this I count the glory of my crown, that I have reigned with your loves. This makes me that I do not so much rejoice, that God hath made me to be a Queen, as, to be a Queen over so thankful a people.

Therefore, I have cause to wish nothing more, than to content the subjects; and that is a duty which I owe: neither do I desire to live longer days, than that I may see your prosperity; and that's my only desire.

And as I am that person, that still (yet under God) hath delivered you; so I trust (by the almighty power of God) that I still shall be his instrument to preserve you from envy, peril, dishonor, shame, tyranny, and oppression; partly by means of your intended helps, which we take very acceptable, because it manifests the largeness of your loves and loyalty to your sovereign.

Of myself, I must say this, I was never any greedy scraping grasper, nor a straight, fast-holding prince, nor yet a waster. My heart was never set on worldly goods, but only for my subjects' good. What you do bestow on me, I will not hoard it up, but receive it to bestow on you again: yea, my own properties I count yours, and to be expended for your good; and your eyes shall see the bestowing of all, for your good. Therefore, render unto them from me, I beseech you, Mr. Speaker, such thanks as you imagine my heart yieldeth, but my tongue cannot express.

> Nota. All this while, we kneeled; whereupon her Majesty said: Mr. Speaker, I would wish you, and the rest to stand up; for I shall yet trouble you with longer speech.
>
> So we all stood up, and she went on with her speech, saying:

Mr. Speaker,

You give me thanks; but I doubt me, that I have more cause to thank you all, than you me. And I charge you, to thank them of the Lower House, from me: for had I not received a knowledge from you, I might have fallen into the lapse of an error, only for lack of true information.

Since I was Queen, yet, did I never put my pen unto any grant, but that, upon pretext and semblance made unto me, it was both good and beneficial to the subject in general; though a private profit to some of my ancient servants, who had deserved well at my hands. But the contrary being found by experience, I am exceedingly beholding to such subjects as would move the same at the first. And I am not so simple to suppose, but that there are some of the Lower House, whom these grievances never touched. And for them, I think they spake out of zeal for the counties, and not out of spleen, or malevolent affection, as being parties grieved. And I take it exceeding gratefully from them; because it gives us to know, that no respects or interests had moved them other than the minds they bear to suffer no diminution of our honor, and our subjects' loves unto us. The zeal of which affection, tending to ease my people, and knit their hearts unto me, I embrace with a princely care; for (above all earthly treasure) I esteem my people's love, more than which I desire not to merit.

That my grants should be grievous to my people, and oppressions privileged under color of our patents; our kingly dignity shall not suffer it: yea, when I heard it, I could give no rest unto my thoughts until I had reformed it.

Shall they think to escape unpunished, that have thus oppressed you, and have been respectless of their duty, and regardless of our honor? No, Mr. Speaker, I assure you, were it not more for conscience-sake, than for any glory or increase of love, that I desire; these errors, troubles, vexations, and oppressions done by these varlets and lewd persons, not worthy the name of subjects, should not escape without condign punishment. But I perceive they dealt with me like physicians, who administering a drug, make it more acceptable by giving it a good aromatical savor, or when they give pills, do gild them all over.

I have ever used to set the last Judgment Day before my eyes as so to rule, as I shall be judged to answer before a higher judge, to whose judgment-seat I do appeal, that never thought was cherished in my heart, that tended not to my people's good. And now, if my kingly bounty have been abused, and my grants turned to the hurt of my people, contrary to my will and meaning; or if any in authority under me, have neglected or perverted what I have committed to them; I hope God will not lay their culps and offences to my charge; who though there were danger in repealing our grants, yet what danger would I not rather incur for your good, than I would suffer them still to continue?

I know the title of a King is a glorious title. But I assure yourself, that the shining glory of princely authority hath not so dazzled the eyes of our understanding; but that we well know and remember that we also are to yield an account of our actions, before the Great Judge.

To be a King, and wear a crown, is a thing more glorious to them that see it, than it is pleasing to them that bear it: for myself, I was never so much enticed with the glorious name of a King, or royal authority of a Queen, as delighted that God had made me his instrument to maintain his truth and glory, and to defend this kingdom (as I said) from peril, dishonor, tyranny, and oppression.

There will never Queen sit in my seat, with more zeal to my country, care for my subjects, and that sooner with willingness will venture her life for your good and safety, than myself. For it is not my desire to live nor reign longer, than my life and reign shall be for your good. And though you have had, and may have many princes, more mighty and wise, sitting in this state; yet you never had, or shall have any that will be more careful and loving.

Shall I ascribe anything to myself, and my sexly weakness? I were not worthy to live then: and of all, most unworthy of the great mercies I have had from God, who hath ever yet given me a heart, which never yet feared foreign or home enemy. I speak it to give God the praise, as a testimony before you, and not to attribute anything to myself. For I, Oh Lord, What am I, whom practices and perils past should not fear? Or, what can I do? [These words she spake with great emphasis.] That I should speak for any glory, God forbid.

This, Mr. Speaker, I pray you deliver to the House, to whom heartily commend me. And so, I commit you all to your best fortunes, and further councils. And I pray you, Mr. Comptroller, Mr. Secretary and you of my Council, that before these gentlemen depart into their counties, you bring them all to kiss my hand. [7]

[7] From Haywood Townsend, *Historical Collections . . . The Four Last Parliaments of Elizabeth* (London, 1680), pp. 248–49, 252, 263–66.

ELIZABETH I IN HISTORY

Since Elizabeth's time, her story has been told and retold in a host of memoirs, biographies, romances, and histories. No one has ever traced the unfolding of this literature through the centuries; it would be a great but valuable labor. Doubtless it would reveal a steady accumulation of knowledge about her life and reign. More than likely, however, it would leave the subtler questions of her character and motives in confusion: for the Queen has been interpreted in many different and sometimes contradictory ways. If some of these appear to us more convincing, none is likely to prove definitive. Each generation, we are reminded, finds its own perspective, and history must continuously be rewritten. But each generation finds its own insights as well, and some of these are presented here. Although only a few examples may be offered, it is hoped that they will define at least some of the interpretive problems and possibilities. The student who wishes to know more may consult the Bibliographical Note.

In the seventeenth century a number of memoirs and biographies appeared. These retain some value as first-hand sources but they must be used thus with caution. Some have already been drawn upon; here are excerpts from two further memoirs, written long after Elizabeth's death by men who had lived through part of her reign. The first is by Robert Naunton (1563–1635) who became a Secretary of State in the next reign. His work was not published until 1641. The second is by Francis Osborne (1593–1659) and did not appear until 1658. These are followed by a critical discussion of the value of the various Elizabethan memoirs to the modern historian. The author, Sir John Neale, is the foremost Elizabethan historian of his generation and has himself written the best modern biography of Elizabeth.

SIR ROBERT NAUNTON, "FRAGMENTA REGALIA" [1]

She was of person tall, of hair and complexion fair, and therewith well favored, but high-nosed; of limbs and features neat, and, which added to the lustre of these external graces, of a stately and majestic comportment, participating in this more of her father than of her mother, who was of an inferior alloy, plausible, or as the French hath it, more debonnaire and affable; virtures, which might well suit with majesty, and which, descending as hereditary to the daughter, did render her of a sweeter temper, and endeared her more to the love and liking of the people, who gave her the name and fame of a most gracious and popular princess.

*   *   *

The principle note of her reign will be, that she ruled much by faction and parties, which she herself both made, upheld, and weakened, as her own great judgment advised; for I do disassent from the common and received opinion, that my Lord of Leicester was absolute and alone in her grace; and, though I come somewhat short of the knowledge of these times, yet, that I may not err, or shoot at random, I know it from assured intelligence that it was not so; for proof whereof amongst many (that could present) I will both relate a story and therein a known truth, and it was thus: Bowyer, the gentleman of the black rod, being charged by her express command, to look precisely to all admissions in the privy-chamber, one day stayed a very gay captain (and follower of my Lord of Leicester) from entrance, for that he was neither well known, nor a sworn servant of the Queen; at which repulse, the gentleman (bearing high on my Lord's favor) told him, that he might, perchance, procure him a discharge. Leicester coming to the contestation said publicly, which was none of his wonted speeches, "that he was a knave, and should not long continue in his office"; and so turning about to go to the Queen, Bowyer, who was a bold gentleman and well beloved, stepped before him, and fell at her Majesty's feet, relates the story, and humbly craves her Grace's pleasure, and in such a manner as if

---

[1] From Sir Robert Naunton, "Fragmenta Regalia," in *Harleian Miscellany*, ed. Thomas Park (London, 1813), II, 82–86.

he had demanded, whether my Lord of Leicester was king, or her Majesty, queen; whereunto she replied (with her wonted oath), "God's-death, my Lord, I have wished you well, but my favor is not so locked up for you, that others shall not participate thereof; for I have many servants unto whom I have and will, at my pleasure, bequeath my favor, and likewise resume the same; and if you think to rule here, I will take a course to see you forthcoming: I will have here but one mistress, and no master; and look that no ill happen to him, lest it be severely required at your hands": which so quailed my Lord of Leicester, that his faint humility was, long after, one of his best virtues.

Moreover, the Earl of Sussex, then Lord Chamberlain, was his professed antagonist, to his dying-day; and for my Lord Hunsdon, and Sir Thomas Sackville, after Lord Treasurer, who were all contemporaries, he was wont to say of them, "that they were of the tribe of Dan, and were, *Noli me tangere":* implying that they were not to be contested with, for they were, indeed, of the Queen's nigh kindred.

From whence, and in many more instances, I conclude, that she was absolute and sovereign mistress of her graces, and that all those, to whom she distributed her favor, were never more than tenants at will, and stood on no better terms than her princely pleasure, and their good behavior. And this also I present as a known observation, that she was, though very capable of counsel, absolute enough in her own resolution; which was ever apparent even to her last, and in that of her still aversion to grant Tyrone the least drop of her mercy, though earnestly and frequently advised thereunto; yea, wrought only by her whole council of state, with very many reasons; and, as the state of her kingdom then stood (I may speak it with assurance) necessitated arguments.

If we look into her inclination as it was disposed to magnificence or frugality, we shall find in them many notable considerations; for all her dispensations were so poised, as though discretion and justice had both decreed to stand at the beam, and see them weighed out in due proportion, the maturity of her paces and judgments meeting in a concurrence; and that in such an age that seldom lapseth to excess.

To consider them apart, we have not many precedents of her

liberality, nor any large donatives to particular men; my Lord of Essex's book of parks excepted, which was a princely gift; and some more of a lesser size, to my Lord of Leicester, Hatton, and others. Her rewards chiefly consisted in grants and leases of offices and places of judicature, but for ready money, and in great sums, she was very sparing: which we may partly conceive, was a virtue rather drawn out of necessity than her nature; for she had many layings-out, and as her wars were lasting, so their charge increased to the last period. And I am of opinion with Sir Walter Ralegh, that those many brave men of her times and of the militia, tasted little more of her bounty, than in her grace and good word with their due entertainment: for she ever paid her soldiers well, which was the honor of her times, and more than her great adversary of Spain could perform; so that, when we come to the consideration of her frugality, the observation will be little more, than that her bounty and it were so woven together, that the one was stained by an honorable way of sparing.

*   *   *

But, to our purpose: The Queen was now to learn, that, as the strength of the kingdom consisted in the multitude of her subjects, so the security of her person consisted and rested in the love and fidelity of her people, which she politically affects (as it hath been thought) somewhat beneath the height of her natural spirit and magnanimity. Moreover, it will be a true note of her providence, that she would always listen to her profit. For she would not refuse the information of meanest personages, which proposed improvement; and had learned the philosophy of (*Hoc agere*) to look unto her own work: of which there is a notable example of one Carmarthen, an under-officer of the custom-house; who, observing his time, presented her with a paper, showing how she was abused in the under-renting of the customs, and therewith humbly desired her Majesty to conceal him, for that it did concern two or three of her great counsellors, whom customer Smith had bribed with two thousand pounds a man, so to lose the Queen twenty thousand pounds per annum; which being made known to the Lords, they gave strict order that Carmarthen should not have access to the back-stairs: but, at last, her Majesty smelling the craft, and missing Carmarthen, she sent for him back, and encouraged him to stand to his information; which the poor man did so handsomely, that, within the space of ten years, he was brought to double his rent, or leave the custom to new farmers. So that we may take this also in consideration, that there were of the Queen's counsel, which were not in the catalogue of saints.

FRANCIS OSBORNE [2]

Now as wisdom and secrecy appeared in her Counsel Chamber so hospitality, charity and splendor were dilated over the whole Court; where, upon the least acquaintance, all strangers from the noble man to the peasant, were invited to one table or other (of which she kept abundance, wherever she removed from one standing house to another, unless she returned to White Hall at night) the least considerable sitting with three, four, or five hundred pounds per annum expense, and for bread, beer and wine (commonly called by the name of budge) though the purveyors that brought it in, were called to strict accounts, such as issued them out were rarely questioned, but in case they sold it: and by this generosity the ordinary sort of people were so endeared as I have known some brag of their entertainment at Court twenty years after. Such like dogs seldom biting those that have once fed them, though with the same meat they have been at the pains to catch themselves, it coming all out of the country man's barns or yards, the wine being little when custom was abated.

Yet though she was thus plentifully provided of all things at home, she did not seldom fetch an entertainment at such grandees' houses as were understood to be most popular. By which she removed her subjects' eyes from intending wholly the influence of these inferior stars, and fixed them upon a greater splendor of her own: besides her out-doing them in the art of popularity, acting to the life the pageant of the people (which all princes really are, and the wisest the most gaudy) from whence it is far more endearing to throw flowers than wild-fire. And if this her affability did not work upon the will, the greatness of their expense did not fail to render them less able to hurt. And in case this was not sufficient to moderate their ambitious thirst

[2] From Francis Osborne, *Historical Memoires* (London, 1658), pp. 54–55, 66.

after popularity, she found them diversions in foreign employments whither they were sent ambassadors or agents, by which their estates were gelt, and the owners rendered the less rampant and unable to maintain their former bewitching humor of hospitality; so as in Parliaments they became assertors of the profit of the Crown, in hope to have such debts refunded as had been contracted by themselves in the service of the State; whose honor she preserved at the lowest expense that ever prince did, and not seldom at their charge who might otherwise have employed their revenues in formenting sedition.

* * *

No prince then extant took an exacter estimate of her subjects' liberties to serve her, or made a deeper inspection into their aptitude, nature and humors; to which with rare dexterity she fitted her favors and their employments: as may be instanced in Francis Vere, a man nobly descended, Walter Ralegh exactly qualified with many others set apart in her judgment for military services, whose titles she never raised above Knighthood; saying when importuned to make general Vere a Baron that, in his proper sphere and in her estimation he was above it already; therefore all could be expected from such an addition, would be entombing of the spirit of a brave soldier in the corpse of a less sightly courtier, and by tempting him from his charge, hazard that repute upon a carpet, his valor had dearly purchased in the field. Nor could she endure to see her subjects wear titles of a foreign prince, the cause she committed Sir Matthew Arundel of Warder in the West, for accepting from the German Caesar the dignity of a Count, and denied Sir Philip Sidney the Crown of Poland.

SIR JOHN NEALE [3]

. . . so far as I know there has hitherto been no attempt to set up a canon and apocrypha of stories. The reason is simple. It would involve elaborate criticism of a hundred and one books, and even

[3] From Sir John Neale, "The Sayings of Queen Elizabeth," in *History*, X (1925), 219–20, 221–23, 223–24, 227–29. Reprinted in *Essays in Elizabethan History* (London, 1958). Reprinted here by permission of Jonathan Cape Limited and St. Martin's Press, Inc.

then we could say no more than "probable" or "improbable" about most of the stories. Such criticism I do not pretend for a moment to have undertaken; but in the remaining pages of this article I hope to make a preliminary essay towards a differentiation between the true and false in regard to a few of the reputed sayings and stories.

It goes almost without saying that some are apocryphal. Wit was in fashion at the Court of Elizabeth, as it is in a community like Oxford, and we hardly need reminding that the men of established reputation in such circles are often strangers to their own foster-lings. At the peace conference of 1919, where there was a company of experts adept at word-play and a few statesmen at the centre of things distinguished politically and not incapable of a bon mot, we are told that the epigrams which were invented were fathered with astonishing regularity upon the same few, and especially upon M. Clémenceau. It would be difficult to say what mordant epigrams Clémenceau was responsible for, and what not; and equally difficult is it, and for the same reasons, to tell what sayings were really Eliz-abeth's. Her wit was equal to them all. She was a woman of ready and vigorous mind and considerable culture, and the figurative style of her writing and speaking gave her excellent practice in turning phrases. She loved metaphor and simile, antithesis and epigram, and sometimes got herself so involved in her conceits that her listeners and correspondents must have been as perplexed about her meaning as her statesmen were. "No man can knowe the inward entencyon of her harte . . . but God and her selfe," said her councillors when consulted about the Anjou marriage negotiations; and Walsingham, when advising the Queen on the same project, wisely wrote, "If you mean it. . . . If you mean it not."

*   *   *

Now how can historical science, or, to use Lord Bryce's less pre-tentious phrase, refined common sense, hope to separate the false from the true in the traditional stories about such a woman as this? *Omnis fabula fundatur in historia,* it has been said. Perhaps; but we must examine the foundations, none the less; and it is only by a critical review of our sources that our problem will be solved, if at all. Let me illustrate the point by examining one of the best known of Elizabethan stories. In 1566 Sir James Melville was sent to England by Mary Queen of Scots to announce the birth of her child. Melville tells us in his *Memoirs* that Cecil first whispered the news to Elizabeth in the course of a dance. Thereupon "all her mirth was laid aside for that night," and sitting down she put her hand under her cheek and burst out with the moan "that the Queen of Scots was Mother of a fair son, while she was but a barren stock."

"When men's memories do arise," said Fuller, who was himself a delightfully garrulous offender, "it is time for History to haste to bed." Melville's *Memoirs* were the child of his old age, and though he had some of his papers by him on which to rely, fickle memory played its tricks, and his narrative is by no means reliable. If not conclusive proof that this particular story is false, it is at least sufficient to make us pause in believing it, that the Spanish ambassador, Silva, who was not at all one to miss the chance of re-tailing such a story, and who saw Melville the day after his audi-ence, merely tells Philip that "the Queen seemed very glad of the birth of the infant": nor had he a different tale to tell, though he was an assiduous collector of Court gossip, when he wrote again four days later. Other stories go back to Melville for their parent-age, the best known of which is probably the amusing debate which he says took place between Elizabeth and himself in 1564, on the relative accomplishments and qualities of his mistress and herself. We cannot say that its pedigree is above suspicion and we cannot test it, although I confess a sneaking desire to keep the tale.

Few of the Queen's sayings are so choice, though their charm de-pends upon their setting rather than any intrinsic brilliance, as are those connected with her progresses. The supreme moments of her genius were these, and if with their masques and verses her progresses belong to the history of the drama, they are no less part of the unwritten story of government propaganda. Old age failed to cloy her appetite for them, and we find her in her sixty-seventh year resolutely determined to go on her long progress to Totten-ham, and with fine spirit replying to the lords who were grumbling at the prospect of the fatigue, by bidding "the old stay behind, and the young and able to goe with her." The accounts we have of these progresses are strictly contemporary, written generally immedi-ately after the events, by eye-witnesses. Some are printed tracts, and their sale surely fostered that popular interest in Elizabeth which made her the symbol of a quickening national consciousness. Their evidence is not beyond cavil. Narrators could not have heard all they report. Some of the Queen's sayings must have come from the story of the visit which immediately gained currency in the neighborhood; and perhaps the writers no less than the simple folk who constructed the epic in their taverns, did not leave the tale unadorned.

*   *   *

I give free rein to scepticism when we come to our next two sources. They are Bacon's *Apophthegms*, and Fuller's *Worthies*. In both, wit or love of a good story prompted most of the tales, and Clio must needs cover her face and hide her blushes, for the inveterate raconteur is without scruple. Everything was fish that came into Fuller's net. His "bare skeleton of time, place, and person, must," he confessed, "be fleshed with some pleasant passages"; and consequently he "purposely interlaced . . . many delightful stories, that so the Reader, if he do not arise . . . religiosior or doctior . . . , at least he may depart jucundior." He is not a contemporary authority (he was born in 1608), and even supposing we could believe that his traditional stories had contemporary origins, their parentage would still be doubtful. The *onus probandi* is on the narrator when merry tales are in doubt.

From Fuller come two stories about Sir Walter Ralegh at which one cannot but strain. The first is the famous story of the new plush cloak which he spread in the mud to keep the Queen's feet from being soiled, by his gallantry winning her attention and favor, and gaining, as it has been punningly said, many good suits by the spoiling of a cloak. Where Fuller got the story from I do not know. Naunton, a younger contemporary of Ralegh's, does not tell the tale, apt though it would have been in his *Fragmenta Regalia*, and I am inclined to think that it was the invention of a later generation wishing to explain so rapid a rise to favor. As an explanation it has the misfortune to be needless. Ralegh may have been introduced at Court by Katherine Ashley, a relative of his, or by the Earl of Leicester, and being a man of good parts, mentally and physically, a ready talker and a wit, an introduction was sufficient to make him free of a company loving pride of life, "the cowrtes vanitie, ambition's puff ball," for, as Fuller puts it, the Queen well knew *Gratior est pulchro veniens e corpore virtus*. The other story belongs to his early days at Court and tells that he wrote on a glass window, "Fain would I climb, yet fear to fall." Upon seeing it, the Queen completed the distich by subscribing, "If thy heart fails thee, climb not at all." It is impossible, and naturally so, to show that a tale of this sort is apocryphal; but if we set out to credit all that we cannot disprove, we shall write strange history, and I am content to state my argument as frank scepticism. Other sayings of the Queen rest upon the uncertain authority of Fuller, amongst which is her reply to Burghley's servant when he bade her stoop as she entered the door at Burghley House to visit the sick minister: "For your Master's sake I will stoop," she is made to say; "but not for the King of Spain's." This also I would put in our apocrypha.

Bacon's *Apophthegms* contain quite a number of Elizabethan stories, amongst which are some of the Queen's sayings. Most of the apophthegms were dictated from memory by Bacon in 1624. Others appeared only after his death, and though it is probable that they were copied from his papers, one cannot be quite certain of it. Supposing, however, that we accept Bacon's authority for these stories, we must still remember that in collecting them he was not concerned with their historical accuracy, but with their wit or moral, and accordingly neither his scholarly sense nor his position in Elizabethan society can be held to establish the stories as genuine. Only when he was himself an ear-witness need we receive them into our established canon. . . .

Between Bacon and Sir John Harington there may seem to be little to choose in the way of reliability, and that little in Bacon's favor: I draw a distinction, resting not upon the qualities of the men but upon the character of those writings of theirs in which sayings of the Queen are found. Unsatisfying as the editing of Harington's papers is in *Nugae Antiquae*, they still are his private papers, consisting of letters and diary entries as well as of more definitely literary pieces; and Harington was well placed both to hear himself and to learn of others when the Queen shone in repartee. His parents had earned the gratitude of Elizabeth by their service to her in the perilous days of Mary, a service which brought them into prison; and when their son John was born in 1561 the

Queen repaid their loyalty by standing as godmother to him. As the boy grew he became welcome at Court, not alone as the Queen's godson, but as a wit of no small repute. Consequently his tales, when no appreciable time intervenes before their telling, carry a certain weight; but he was too much the established wit to look closely at a good story, and the value of his evidence diminishes considerably when he is engaged upon a literary composition like his *Briefe View of the State of the Church.*

*   *   *

Legend clouds over us as we turn from the incidents of the Queen's life to those of her death, for there is a dramatic sense in popular story which demands of its famous people that they shall die fittingly, so acquitting themselves on their deathbeds as to point a moral or adorn a tale. The biographer of Elizabeth may, like Mr. Chamberlain, choose as the Queen's last words a highly moral reflection—"My lord, the crown which I have borne so long has given enough of vanity in my time"; or he may finish his portrait of a frivolous woman with the cry, "A million of money for a moment of time": only, if he does, he will be the dupe, in the latter instance of someone, I know not whom, and in the former of the egregious Leti. Mr. Chamberlain devotes four pages of his book to the sayings of what he calls "the inevitable hour." I might dispose of most of them by an individual examination of their sources, but such a method of attack would be involved and wasteful, and it will be more useful and equally effective if I review the various accounts of Elizabeth's death, separating the reliable from the unreliable.

One counsel of safety there is in such a review, and one only— to start from strictly contemporary narratives, that is, from letters written actually during the illness. Much the most informative are the dispatches of the French ambassador, Beaumont, who evidently drew his bulletins from the Court, despite the fact that Cecil and the Council, nourished on an inherited fear of what might befall at the Queen's death, were at first doing their best to prevent news leaking out and alarming the country. It is an ordinary death-bed tale that the dispatches tell, unadorned by terrible visions and with few random flashes of Elizabethan temper. Unable to sleep, parched in throat and body, and plunged in a deep melancholy; refusing for days to enter what she instinctively felt would be her death-bed, spurning medicine, and having little taste for food, the Queen gradually sank, plagued by the solicitations of doctors and councillors, until she passed into a stupor and the end came. Chamberlain, writing to Carleton on March 30th—the Queen died in the early hours of March 24th—says nothing more; and the moment we venture beyond some such general outline to fill in any details, especially of words which Elizabeth may have spoken, we are in a whirl of uncertainty, for gossip got to work immediately. "Even here," says Chamberlain, writing six days after her death, "the papists do tell strange stories as utterly voyde of truth, as of all civill honestie or humanitie."

One problem with which I must deal, before examining the set narratives of Elizabeth's death, is whether she did or did not name a successor. There is no hint that she did in any letter written during her illness. Beaumont appears to have been in touch with the Earl of Northumberland, and was told by him in all secrecy that the councillors had determined to proclaim James the moment Elizabeth was dead; but as late as the day following her death he states definitely that she had named no successor. Eleven days later his news was different. Nottingham and Cecil had seen him and had told him that a few days before her death Elizabeth had said to them in confidence that she recognized no other successor but James, and did not want her kingdom to fall into the hands of rascals. When they later asked her to confirm this before other councillors, being speechless she made a sign by putting her hand to her head. The story may be true. Cecil certainly did announce that Elizabeth had named James as her successor; and perhaps we should believe him. But one contemporary at least looked a little askance at the tale, and it may be that it was an invention given currency after Elizabeth's death to justify the action of the Council. It has found its way into the narratives of her death, sometimes with elaborations.

Of these narratives the most sober and the best known is Sir Robert Carey's. Carey was about the Court during Elizabeth's illness, waiting for the moment when he was to set forth on his famous ride to Edinburgh, harbinger of a flock of time-servers hastening north to worship the newly risen sun. He saw the Queen twice during her last days, and, apart from his own knowledge, had a sister in waiting on Elizabeth and a brother at Court, from whom to draw further information. His narrative, I have said, is sober. It contains one remark of the Queen's only. Its sobriety makes it an admirable check on other accounts; for considering what his sources of information were, and considering also that he did not write his *Memoirs* until about 1627, by which time the legend of Elizabeth's death was practically complete, his deliberate rejection of the details which we find in other narratives—"false lies," he termed them—is strong argument against their authenticity.

Since William Camden's attempt early in the seventeenth century, the narrative historians have often turned to the reign of Elizabeth to reinterpret it. In the nineteenth century two men of very different religious persuasions made original and important contributions to the study of the Queen, John Lingard (1771–1851) and James Anthony Froude (1818–1894). Lingard devoted an entire volume of his History of England *to her reign, writing from a moderate Catholic point of view. He wished to refute earlier writers like David Hume, without repelling his Protestant readers. Lingard wrote to his publisher that although Elizabeth did not appear in his work as "a very amiable character" he had set nothing down in malice and sought to be impartial. His work was very popular; it concludes with the character sketch given below. Froude's* History of England from the Fall of Wolsey to the Spanish Armada *may be considered a response to Lingard and others. Its original 12 volumes (six on Elizabeth) incorporated much new material and a vivid style. It swiftly became an historical classic despite inaccuracies and a strong apologetic tone. Nevertheless Froude took an increasingly dim view of Elizabeth and gave most of the credit for the achievements of the reign to Burghley. Part of his concluding chapter is given here.*

JOHN LINGARD [4]

From the elevation of the throne, we may now follow her into the privacy of domestic life. Her natural abilities were great; she had studied under experienced masters; and her stock of literature was much more ample than that of most females of the age. Like her sister Mary, she possessed a knowledge of five languages; but Mary did not venture to converse in Italian, neither could she construe the Greek Testament, like Elizabeth. The queen is said to have excelled on the virginals, and to have understood the most difficult music. But dancing was her principal delight; and in that exercise she displayed a grace and spirit which was universally admired. . . .

Of her vanity the reader will have noticed several instances in the preceding pages. . . .

The courtiers soon discovered how greedy their sovereign was of flattery. If they sought to please, they were careful to admire; and adulation the most fulsome and extravagant was accepted by the queen with gratitude, and rewarded with bounty. Neither was her appetite for praise cloyed, it seemed rather to become more craving by enjoyment. After she had passed her grand climacteric, she exacted the same homage to her faded charms as had been paid to her youth and all who addressed her were still careful to express their admiration of her beauty in the language of oriental hyperbole.

But however highly she might think of her person, she did not despise the aid of external ornament. At her death, two, some say three, thousand dresses were found in her wardrobe, with a numerous collection of jewelery, for the most part presents which she had received from petitioners, from her courtiers on her saint's day, and at the beginning of each year, and from the noblemen and gentlemen whose houses she had honored with her presence. To the austere notions of the bishop of London, this love of finery appeared unbecoming her age, and in his sermon he endeavoured to raise her thoughts from the ornaments of dress to the riches of

[4] From John Lingard, *The History of England*, 6th ed. (London, 1855), VI, 320–24.

Heaven; but she told her ladies, that if he touched upon that subject again, she would fit *him* for Heaven. He should walk there without a staff, and leave his mantle behind him.

In her temper Elizabeth seemed to have inherited the irritability of her father. The least inattention, the slightest provocation, would throw her into a passion. At all times her discourse was sprinkled with oaths; in the sallies of her anger it abounded with imprecations and, abuse. Nor did she content herself with words; not only the ladies about her person, but her courtiers and the highest officers in the state, felt the weight of her hands. She collared Hatton, she gave a blow on the ear to the earl marshal, and she spat on Sir Matthew Arundel, with the foppery of whose dress she was offended.

To her first parliament she had expressed a wish that on her tomb might be inscribed the title of "the virgin queen." But the woman who despises the safeguards must be content to forfeit the reputation of chastity. It was not long before her familiarity with Dudley provoked dishonourable reports. At first they gave her pain; but her feelings were soon blunted by passion; in the face of the whole court she assigned to her supposed paramour an apartment contiguous to her own bed-chamber; and by this indecent act proved that she was become regardless of her character, and callous to every sense of shame. But Dudley, though the most favoured, was not considered as her only lover; among his rivals were numbered Hatton, and Ralegh, and Oxford, and Blount, and Simier, and Anjou; and it was afterwards believed that her licentious habits survived, even when the fire of wantonness had been quenched by the chill of age. The court imitated the manners of the sovereign. It was a place in which, according to Faunt, "all enormities reigned in the highest degree," or according to Harington, "where there was no love, but that of the lusty god of gallantry, Asmodeus."

Elizabeth firmly believed and zealously upheld the principles of government established by her father—the exercise of absolute authority by the sovereign, and the duty of passive obedience in the subject. . . .

*   *   *

The queen was not sparing of the blood of her subjects. The statutes inflicting death for religious opinion have been . . . noticed. In addition, many new felonies and new treasons were created during her reign; and the ingenuity of the judges gave to these enactments the most extensive application. In 1595 some apprentices in London conspired to release their companions, who had been condemned by the Star-chamber to suffer punishment for a riot; in 1597 a number of peasants in Oxfordshire assembled to break down inclosures, and restore tillage; each of these offences, as it opposed the execution of the law, was pronounced treason by the judges; and both the apprentices in London, and the men of Oxfordshire, suffered the barbarous death of traitors.

JAMES ANTHONY FROUDE [5]

Elizabeth's situation was from the very first extremely trying. She had few relations, none of any weight in the State, and those whom like Hunsdon and Sir Francis Knowles she took into her Cabinet, derived their greatness from herself. Her unlucky, it may be almost called culpable, attachment to Leicester made marriage unconquerably distasteful to her, and her disappointment gave an additional twist to her natural eccentricities. Circumstances more than choice threw her originally on the side of the Reformation, and when she told the Spanish ambassadors that she had been forced into the separation from the Papacy against her will, she probably spoke but the truth. She was identified in her birth with the cause of independence. The first battle had been fought over her cradle, and her right to be on the throne turned morally, if not in law, on the legitimacy of Queen Catherine's divorce. Her sister had persecuted her as the child of the woman who had caused her mother so much misery, and her friends therefore had naturally been those who were most her sister's enemies. She could not have submitted to the Pope without condemning her father, or admitting a taint upon her own birth, while in Mary of Scotland she had a rival ready to take advantage of any concession which she might be tempted to make.

For these reasons, and not from any sympathy with the views either of Luther or Calvin, she chose her party at her accession. She found herself compelled against her will to become the patron

[5] From James Anthony Froude, *History of England from the Fall of Wolsey to the Defeat of the Spanish Armada* (London, 1870), XII, 505-9, 510.

of heretics and rebels, in whose objects she had no interest, and in whose theology she had no belief. She resented the necessity while she submitted to it, and her vacillations are explained by the reluctance with which each successive step was forced upon her, on a road which she detested. It would have been easy for a Protestant to be decided. It would have been easy for a Catholic to be decided. To Elizabeth the speculations of so-called divines were but as ropes of sand and sea-slime leading to the moon, and the doctrines for which they were rending each other to pieces a dream of fools or enthusiasts. Unfortunately her keenness of insight was not combined with any profound concern for serious things. She saw through the emptiness of the forms in which religion presented itself to the world. She had none the more any larger or deeper conviction of her own. She was without the intellectual emotions which give human character its consistency and power. One moral quality she possessed in an eminent degree: she was supremely brave. For thirty years she was perpetually a mark for assassination, and her spirits were never affected, and she was never frightened into cruelty. She had a proper contempt also for idle luxury and indulgence. She lived simply, worked hard, and ruled her household with rigid economy. But her vanity was as insatiable as it was commonplace. No flattery was too tawdry to find a welcome with her, and as she had no repugnance to false words in others, she was equally liberal of them herself. Her entire nature was saturated with artifice. Except when speaking some round untruth Elizabeth never could be simple. Her letters and her speeches were as fantastic as her dress, and her meaning as involved as her policy. She was unnatural even in her prayers, and she carried her affectations into the presence of the Almighty. She might doubt legitimately whether she ought to assist an Earl of Murray or a Prince of Orange when in arms against their Sovereign; but her scruples extended only to the fulfilment of her promises of support, when she had herself tempted them into insurrection. Obligations of honor were not only occasionally forgotten by her, but she did not seem to understand what honor meant.

Vain as she was of her own sagacity, she never modified a course recommended to her by Burghley without injury both to the realm and to herself. She never chose an opposite course without plunging into embarrassments, from which his skill and Walsingham's were barely able to extricate her. The great results of her reign were the fruits of a policy which was not her own, and which she starved and mutilated when energy and completeness were most needed.

That she pushed no question to extremities, that, for instance, she refused to allow the succession to the crown to be determined, and permitted the Catholics to expect the accession of the Queen of Scots, has been interpreted by the result into wisdom. She gained time by it, and her hardest problems were those which time alone could resolve satisfactorily. But the fortune which stood her friend so often never served her better than in lengthening her life into old age. Had the Queen of Scots survived her, her legacy to England would have been a desperate and dreadful civil war. And her reluctance was no result of any farsighted or generous calculation. She wished only to reign in quiet till her death, and was contented to leave the next generation to settle its own difficulties. Her tenderness towards conspirators was as remarkable as it was hitherto unexampled; but her unwillingness to shed blood extended only to high-born traitors. Unlike her father, who ever struck the leaders and spared the followers, Elizabeth could rarely bring herself to sign the death-warrant of a nobleman; yet without compunction she could order Yorkshire peasants to be hung in scores by martial law. Mercy was the quality with which she was most eager to be credited. She delighted in popularity with the multitude, and studied the conditions of it; but she uttered no word of blame, she rather thanked the perpetrators for good service done to the commonwealth, when Essex sent in his report of the women and children who were stabbed in the caves of Rathlin. She was remorseless when she ought to have been most forbearing, and lenient when she ought to have been stern; and she owed her safety and her success to the incapacity and the divisions of her enemies, rather than to wisdom and resolution of her own. Time was her friend, time and the weakness of Philip; and the fairest feature in her history, the one relation in which from first to last she showed sustained and generous feeling, is that which the perversity of history has selected as the blot on her escutcheon. Beyond and beside the political causes which influenced Elizabeth's attitude towards the Queen of Scots, true human pity, true kindness, a true desire to save her from herself, had a real place. . . . It seems as if Elizabeth, remembering her own danger in her sister's life-time, had studied to show an elaborate tenderness to a person who was in the same relation to herself. From the beginning to the end no trace can be found of personal animosity on the part of Elizabeth; on the part of Mary no trace of anything save the fiercest hatred.

But this, like all other questions connected with the Virgin Queen, should be rather studied in her actions than in the opinion of the historian who relates them. Actions and words are carved upon eternity. Opinions are but forms of cloud created by the prevailing currents of the moral air. Princes, who are credited on the wrong side with the evils which happen in their reigns, have a right in equity to the honour of the good. The greatest achievement in English history, the "breaking the bonds of Rome," and the establishment of spiritual independence, was completed without bloodshed under Elizabeth's auspices, and Elizabeth may have the glory of the work. . . .

Since the seventeenth century, Elizabeth has had two kinds of biography. There have been works written by serious historians (academic or otherwise) and there have been works written by essentially literary people or by amateurs. Both have made contributions, although sometimes more to legend than to literal truth. The contrast between Edmund Bohun's Character of Queen Elizabeth *(1693) and Gregorio Leti's romantic biography, the* Historia . . . di Elisabetta *(1694) has repeated itself often, with various gradations between. We have room for only two recent examples here. In 1896 Bishop Mandell Creighton published a short biography of Elizabeth that is a model of its kind. Creighton was a distinguished historian, a founder of the* English Historical Review *and the author of a multivolume* History of the Papacy. *Next to Neale, his biography is probably the best modern life. Some years later Lytton Strachey, renowned for setting a whole new fashion in biography with his* Eminent Victorians, *turned to Elizabeth. Strachey was not a scholar, and was misled about Elizabeth's health by an eccentric study published some years before. But his portrait of the Queen remains a brilliant and suggestive literary sketch.*

MANDELL CREIGHTON [6]

The character of Elizabeth is difficult to detach from her actions. She represented England as no other ruler ever did. For the greater part of her long reign the fortunes of England absolutely depended upon her life, and not only the fortunes of England, but those of Europe as well. If England had passed under the Papal sway it is hard to see how Protestantism could have survived the repressive forces to which it would have been exposed. There were times when Elizabeth doubted if this could be avoided, times when any one, save Anne Boleyn's daughter, would have been tempted to make terms. In asking England to rally round her Elizabeth knew that she could not demand any great sacrifices on her behalf. By cultivating personal loyalty, by demanding it in exaggerated forms, she was not merely feeding her personal vanity; she was creating a habit which was necessary for the maintenance of her government. By avoiding risky undertakings, by keeping down public expense, she was not merely indulging her tendency to parsimony; she was warding off from her people demands which they were unequal at that time to sustain.

Elizabeth's imperishable claim to greatness lies in her instinctive sympathy with her people. She felt, rather than understood, the possibilities which lay before England, and she set herself the task of slowly exhibiting, and impressing them on the national mind. She educated Englishmen to a perception of England's destiny, and for this purpose fixed England's attention upon itself. She caught at every advantage which was afforded by the divided condition of Europe to assert England's importance. France and Spain alike had deep causes of hostility; she played off one against the other, so that both were anxious for the friendship of a State which they each hoped some day to annex. England gained courage from this sight and grew in self-confidence. To obtain this result Elizabeth was careless of personal dignity or honor. She did not care how her conduct was judged at the time, but awaited the result.

It is this faculty of intuitive sympathy with her people which

[6] From Mandell Creighton, *Queen Elizabeth* (London, 1899), pp. 303–7.

makes Elizabeth so difficult to understand in details of her policy. The fact was that she never faced a question in the shape in which it presented itself. It was true that it had to be recognised and discussed in that form; but Elizabeth had no belief in a policy because it could be clearly stated and promised well. Things had to be discussed, and decisions arrived at in consequence of such discussion; but action could always be avoided at the last moment, and Elizabeth would never act unless she felt that her people were in hearty agreement with her. Thus in her position towards her ministers she represented in her own person the vacillations and fluctuations of popular opinion. Ministers naturally wish to have an intelligible policy. Burghley laboriously drew up papers which balanced the advantages and disadvantages of alternative courses of action. Elizabeth read them and seemed to accept one out of two inevitable plans. She felt that, as a reasonable being, she could not do otherwise. But when it came to decisive action she fell back upon her instinctive perception of what England wanted. As she could not explain this, she was driven to all sorts of devices to gain time. She could not, on the other hand, fully take her people into her confidence. It was the unconscious tendency of their capacities which she interpreted, not their actual demands. She was eliciting from them their meaning, and educating them to understand it themselves. For this purpose she must seem to govern more absolutely than she did; but, on great occasions, she took them into her confidence, and fired them with a high conception of the greatness of their national life. She strove to focus and co-ordinate all their aspirations, and only repressed tendencies which were adverse to the formation of an English spirit; for she cared more for the spirit of the national life than for its outward organisation.

Her private character is hard to detach from her public character. She behaved to those around her as she did to her people in general. She was surrounded by men representative of English life; they must be made to fall into line; and any method which served this purpose was good. Above all things she must impose her will equally on all. Personally, she was attracted by physical endowments, and let herself go in accordance with her feelings up to a certain point. But she was both intellectually and emotionally cold. In politics and in private life alike she cared little for decorum, because she knew that she could stop short whenever prudence made it needful.

It is easy to point out serious faults in Elizabeth, to draw out her inconsistencies, and define her character in a series of paradoxes. But this treatment does not exhibit the real woman, still less the real Queen. Elizabeth was hailed at her accession as being "mere English," and "mere English" she remained. Round her, with all her faults, the England which we know grew into the consciousness of its destiny. The process was difficult; the struggle was painful, and it left many scars behind. There are many things in Elizabeth which we could have wished otherwise; but she saw what England might become, and nursed it into the knowledge of its power.

LYTTON STRACHEY [7]

The lion heart, the splendid gestures—such heroic things were there, no doubt—visible to everybody; but their true significance in the general scheme of her character was remote and complicated. The sharp and hostile eyes of the Spanish ambassadors saw something different; in their opinion, the outstanding characteristic of Elizabeth was pusillanimity. They were wrong; but they perceived more of the truth than the idle onlooker. They had come into contact with those forces in the Queen's mind which proved, incidentally, fatal to themselves, and brought her, in the end, her enormous triumph. That triumph was not the result of heroism. The very contrary was the case: the grand policy which dominated Elizabeth's life was the most unheroic conceivable; and her true history remains a standing lesson for melodramatists in statecraft. In reality, she succeeded by virtue of all the qualities which every hero should be without—dissimulation, pliability, indecision, proscrastination, parsimony. It might almost be said that the heroic element chiefly appeared in the unparalleled lengths to which she allowed those qualities to carry her. It needed a lion heart indeed to spend twelve years in convincing the world that she was in love with the Duke of Anjou, and to stint the victuals

[7] From Lytton Strachey, *Elizabeth and Essex* (New York, 1928), pp. 11–15. Copyright © 1928 by Lytton Strachey; renewed 1956 by James Strachey. Reprinted by permission of Harcourt, Brace & World, Inc., Chatto & Windus Ltd., and Mrs. A. S. Strachey.

of the men who defeated the Armada; but in such directions she was in very truth capable of everything. She found herself a sane woman in a universe of violent maniacs, between contending forces of terrific intensity—the rival nationalisms of France and Spain, the rival religions of Rome and Calvin; for years it had seemed inevitable that she should be crushed by one or other of them, and she had survived because she had been able to meet the extremes around her with her own extremes of cunning and prevarication. It so happened that the subtlety of her intellect was exactly adapted to the complexities of her environment. The balance of power between France and Spain, the balance of factions in France and Scotland, the swaying fortunes of the Netherlands, gave scope for a tortuosity of diplomacy which has never been completely unravelled to this day. Burghley was her chosen helper, a careful steward after her own heart; and more than once Burghley gave up the puzzle of his mistress's proceedings in despair. Nor was it only her intellect that served her; it was her temperament as well. That too—its mixture of the masculine and feminine, of vigour and sinuosity, of pertinacity and vacillation—was precisely what her case required. A deep instinct made it almost impossible for her to come to a fixed determination upon any subject whatever. Or, if she did, she immediately proceeded to contradict her resolution with the utmost violence, and, after that, to contradict her contradiction more violently still. Such was her nature—to float, when it was calm, in a sea of indecisions, and, when the wind rose, to tack hectically from side to side. Had it been otherwise—had she possessed, according to the approved pattern of the strong man of action, the capacity for taking a line and sticking to it—she would have been lost. She would have become inextricably entangled in the forces that surrounded her, and, almost inevitably, swiftly destroyed. Her femininity saved her. Only a woman could have shuffled so shamelessly, only a woman could have abandoned with such unscrupulous completeness the last shreds not only of consistency, but of dignity, honour, and common decency, in order to escape the appalling necessity of having, really and truly, to make up her mind. Yet it is true that a woman's evasiveness was not enough; male courage, male energy were needed, if she were to escape the pressure that came upon her from every side. Those qualities she also possessed; but their value to her—it was the final paradox of her career—was merely that they made her strong enough to turn her back, with an indomitable persistence, upon the ways of strength.

Religious persons at the time were distressed by her conduct, and imperialist historians have wrung their hands over her since. Why could she not suppress her hesitations and chicaneries and take a noble risk? Why did she not step forth, boldly and frankly, as the leader of Protestant Europe, accept the sovereignty of Holland, and fight the good fight to destroy Catholicism and transfer the Spanish Empire to the rule of England? The answer is that she cared for none of those things. She understood her true nature and her true mission better than her critics. It was only by an accident of birth that she was a Protestant leader; at heart she was profoundly secular; and it was her destiny to be the champion, not of the Reformation, but of something greater—the Renaissance. When she had finished her strange doings, there was civilisation in England. The secret of her conduct was, after all, a simple one: she had been gaining time. And time, for her purposes, was everything. A decision meant war—war, which was the very antithesis of all she had at heart. Like no other great statesman in history, she was, not only by disposition, but in practice, pacific. It was not that she was much disturbed by the cruelty of war—she was far from sentimental; she hated it for the best of all reasons—its wastefulness. Her thrift was spiritual as well as material, and the harvest that she gathered in was the great Age, to which, though its supreme glories were achieved under her successor, her name has been rightly given. For without her those particular fields could never have come to ripeness; they would have been trodden down by struggling hordes of nationalists and theologians. She kept the peace for thirty years —by dint, it is true, of one long succession of disgraceful collapses and unheard-of equivocations; but she kept it, and that was enough for Elizabeth.

Bibliographical Note

The most important single reference for all matters Elizabethan is Conyers Read's *Bibliography of British History: The Tudor Period 1485–1603* (Oxford, 1959). There is also a concise new bibliography by Mortimer Levine (Cambridge, 1968).

Elizabeth was neither a writer nor a speculative thinker. She did dabble in literature occasionally and some of her translations survive; see *Queen Elizabeth's Englishings,* ed. Caroline Pemberton (Oxford, 1899). She also composed some poetry; a few specimens of which are offered above; see *The Poems of Queen Elizabeth,* ed. Leicester Bradner (Providence, 1964). But her important words and thoughts have to be extracted from a variety of more ephemeral sources, from letters, speeches, and reports of her conversation.

Several thousand letters exist, the great majority of which are official documents. A sample of the more interesting and personal has been edited by G. B. Harrison, *The Letters of Queen Elizabeth* (London, 1935) and most of her early letters appear in Frank Mumby, *The Girlhood of Queen Elizabeth* (London, 1909). There are many older collections that contain letters by the Queen; for example, *Queen Elizabeth and Her Times,* 2 vols., ed. Thomas Wright (London, 1838); *Memoirs of the Reign of Queen Elizabeth,* 2 vols., ed. Thomas Birch (London, 1744); *Original Letters Illustrative of English History,* 3 series, ed. Henry Ellis (London, 1824–1846). And many works print some of her correspondence with particular individuals, several edited by J. Bruce: *The Correspondence of Robert Dudley . . . 1585–6, Letters of Queen Elizabeth and King James VI* (London, 1844, 1849); *Correspondence of Matthew Parker* (London, 1853). See also, *Life and Letters of the Earls of Essex,* 2 vols., ed. Walter Devereux (London, 1853). Elizabeth's correspondence concerning the Austrian match appears, with other documents, in Victor von Klarwill, *Queen Elizabeth and Some*

Foreigners (London, 1928); concerning the French match in *The Compleat Ambassador,* ed. Dudley Digges (London, 1655).

Along with her letters, Elizabeth's speeches hold the greatest interest. A brief selection appears in *The Public Speaking of Queen Elizabeth,* ed. George P. Rice (New York, 1951). More valuable are the speeches given *in extenso* in John Neale, *The Parliaments of Elizabeth,* 2 vols. (London, 1958). These have been freshly edited from manuscripts and include all the known addresses to Parliament. Older collections of parliamentary material are Simonds D'Ewes, *The Journals of all the Parliaments During the Reign of Queen Elizabeth* (London, 1682) and Haywood Townsend, *The Last Four Parliaments of Elizabeth* (London, 1680). The Queen's speeches on her progresses, with much supporting material of all kinds, may be found in *The Progresses and Public Occasions of Queen Elizabeth,* 3 vols., ed. John Nichols (London, 1823). The chronicles (see below) are also useful here.

Elizabeth's conversations were reported in a great variety of sources. Most important are the ambassadors' dispatches, which include invaluable contemporary testimony of all kinds. Many of those are available in calendars of documents issued by the Public Record Office in London. The most useful for Elizabeth are the *Calendars of State Papers Foreign, Spanish, Venetian, Border, and Scottish,* each in many volumes. Much of the French diplomatic correspondence is untranslated but there are useful materials in P. Forbes, ed., *A Full View of the Public Transactions in the Reign of Elizabeth,* 2 vols. (London, 1740); *A Journal of all that was Accomplished by Monsieur de Maisse,* eds. G. B. Harrison and R. A. Jones (London, 1931); *Memoirs of Maximilien de Bethune, Duke of Sully,* trans. Charlotte Lennox, 3 vols. (London, 1756). To these should be added the reports of courtiers and servants, many of which will be found in the *Calendars of State Papers Domestic* and in the *Reports of the Historical Manuscripts Commission,* especially the *Salisbury Manuscripts,* containing the papers of the Cecil family. The texts in the calendars, it must be said, are often abridged and paraphrased. Finally, newsletters and diaries are often useful here. For the former, some examples may be found from the Talbots in ed. E. Lodge, *Illustrations of British History,* 3 vols. (London, 1791); from Roland White in *The Sydney Papers,* 2 vols., ed. A.

Collins (London, 1746); and from various of the Marian reformers to their friends abroad, in *The Zurich Letters,* 2 series, ed. H. Robinson (Parker Soc., 1842, 1845). The two most important diaries are by Henry Machyn, edited by J. G. Nichols; and John Manningham edited by J. Bruce, both for the Camden Society (1848, 1868).

Some important official documents of and about Elizabeth may also be found in the *Harleian Miscellany,* 10 vols. (London, 1808), and *Somers Tracts,* I (London, 1809). Very valuable also are the two volumes comprising *A Collection of State Papers Left by William Cecil,* the first edited by Samuel Haynes for the years 1542–1570 (London, 1740), the second by William Murdin for 1571–1596 (London, 1759). For religious affairs, John Strype's *Annals of the Reformation during Queen Elizabeth's Reign,* 7 vols. (Oxford, 1824) contains much useful primary material.

There are many contemporary accounts of Elizabeth by memoir writers and chroniclers. Most of the former may be traced in the selections above, and some are discussed by Neale (see pp. 151–58). Of the chroniclers, the most important are William Camden, *Annales regnante Elizabetha,* 3 vols., ed. Thomas Hearne (London, 1717); John Stow, *The Annales of England* (London, 1605); Raphael Holinshed, *The Chronicles of England* (London, 1587). Camden was the outstanding Elizabethan historian and his *Annales* employed Cecil's papers and his own observation. They were translated several times; the best English version is the third edition (London, 1675). Holinshed and Stow print many contemporary documents. For the hostile viewpoint, see J. B. Code, *Queen Elizabeth and the English Catholic Historians* (London, 1935).

Of recent biographies of Elizabeth, the most important is Neale's unannotated *Queen Elizabeth* (London, 1934). More recent works are by B. W. Beckingsale and Neville Williams. Still useful is the brief older biography by Bishop Mandell Creighton (London, 1899). More personal than these have been the biographies of the ladies. Lucy Aikin and Agnes Strickland both wrote large works in the last century and quote copiously (if not always accurately) from contemporary documents. Recently, Elizabeth Jenkins has published two biographies interpreting Elizabeth's character in exact, if not entirely convincing, psychological detail, *Elizabeth the Great* (London, 1958) and *Elizabeth and Leicester* (London, 1961).

Of recent histories of the reign, the most famous is James Anthony Froude, *History of England from the Fall of Wolsey to the Spanish Armada*, 12 vols. (London, 1872). This is a classic of English narrative history, vividly written, strongly argued, and therefore often criticized. It includes much primary material which, however, is not always perfectly transcribed. Froude's work was continued, but without the literary flair, by E. P. Cheyney, 2 vols. (New York, 1914–1926). More recent and with valuable bibliographies are A. F. Pollard, *The History of England 1547–1603* (London, 1910) and J. B. Black, *The Reign of Elizabeth* (Oxford, 1959). Pollard's is the best single volume narrative of the reign.

The monographs are too numerous to describe. Read should be employed here, but mention may be made of a few titles. Read himself wrote massive and somewhat tedious biographies of Cecil and Elizabeth, 2 vols. (London and New York, 1956–1960), and Walsingham and Elizabeth, 3 vols. (Oxford, 1925). Neale has written many important essays on the reign, some collected in *Essays in Elizabethan History* (London, 1958). There is also a valuable collection of essays dedicated to him, *Elizabethan Government and Society* (London, 1961). In recent years, Joel Hurstfield has made a number of important contributions, including *Elizabeth and the Unity of England* (London, 1960), and a volume on *The Queen's Wards* (London, 1958). A brief introduction to a crucial subject is Alan Smith's *The Government of Elizabethan England* (London, 1967). Finally for Elizabeth in poetry, there is E. C. Wilson, *England's Eliza* (Cambridge, Mass., 1939), and in painting, Roy C. Strong's *Portraits of Queen Elizabeth* (Oxford, 1963).

Index

A

Act of Supremacy, 68
Act of Uniformity, 68
"Admonitions to Parliament," 80
Alencon, Duc d' (later Duc d'Anjou), 32, 88, 100, 106–10, 167
Anjou, Duc d' (later Henry III), 100, 105, 107, 152, 160
Armada, 41, 57, 62, 65, 79, 83, 91, 122, 124, 168
Arran, Earl of, 100
Arundel, Sir Matthew, 151, 160
Ascham, Roger, "The Schoolmaster," 13
Ashley, Katherine, 154
Audeley, John, "Wonders of England," 23
"Augsburg confession," 85
Aylmer, John, 22, 23

B

Babington plot, 122, 138
Bacon, Anthony, 52, 53
Bacon, Francis, 31, 50, 53, 54, 56, 132, 154, 155
Ballads, 4, 23, 57, 65
Beaumont (French ambassador), 156–57
Bedford, Earl of, 105, 113, 118
Birch, William, 57
Blount, Christopher (Lord Mountjoy), 56, 160
Bohun, Edmund, 164
Boleyn, Anne, 12, 13, 18, 68, 147, 165
"Bond of Association," 123, 124, 129
Bonner, Bishop, 69
Bothwell, Earl of, 118
Boyne, Lady, 117
Bryce, Lord, 152
Buckhurst, Lord, 47
Burghley, Lord, see William Cecil

C

Cadiz, 54
Calvin, John, 21, 81, 161, 168
Cambridge University, 54, 57, 63, 64
Camden, William, 1, 47, 54, 56, 93, 123, 124, 158
Carew, Sir George, 55
Carey, Sir Robert, 1, 38, 40, 157, 158
Catherine of Aragon, 18, 161
Catholics, 3, 7, 41, 69, 73, 75, 76–80, 83, 92, 105, 111, 112, 123, 158, 162, 163, 169
Cecil, Sir Robert, 40, 49, 51, 53, 55, 80, 93, 132, 156, 157
Cecil, William, 6, 21, 31, 35, 42, 43, 47–50, 51, 54, 63, 76, 79, 82, 91, 107, 109, 115, 117, 120, 121, 134, 153, 155, 158, 162, 166, 168
Chamberlain, on Elizabeth, 156
"Chamberlain Letters," 157
Chapuys, Eustace (Imperial ambassador), 12
Charles, Prince of Austria, 100
Cicero, 14, 102
Clapham, John, 1
Council of Trent, 70
Counter-Reformation, 79, 80
Courtenay, Edward, 14, 15
Creighton, Bishop Mandell, on Elizabeth, 164, 165

D

Dacre, Leonard, 76
Darnley, Henry Stuart, Lord, 112, 114, 117, 118
Davison, William, 124, 130
Derby, Countess of, 108
D'Ewes, Sir Simonds, "Journals," 134, 136

174

GREAT LIVES OBSERVED

Gerald Emanuel Stearn, *General Editor*

Other volumes in the series: